MANUAL FOR
CLINICAL
PSYCHOLOGY
TRAINEES

MANUAL FOR CLINICAL PSYCHOLOGY TRAINEES

SECOND EDITION

James P. Choca, Ph.D.

Chief of Psychology, Veterans Administration Lakeside
Hospital at Northwestern University Medical School,
Chicago

BRUNNER/MAZEL, *Publishers* • New York

Library of Congress Cataloging-in-Publication Data

Choca, James.
  Manual for clinical psychology trainees / James P. Choca. — 2nd
ed.
    p. cm.
  Rev. ed. of: Manual for clinical psychology practicums. c1980.
  Bibliography: p.
  ISBN 0-87630-544-3
  1. Clinical psychology—Handbooks, manuals, etc.
  2. Psychodiagnostics—Handbooks, manuals, etc.   3. Psychotherapy—
Handbooks, manuals, etc.   I. Choca, James.   Manual for
clinical psychology practicums.   II. Title.
  [DNLM: 1. Psychology, Clinical.   WM 105 C545m]
  RC467.C46   1988
  616.89—dc19
  DNLM/DLC
  for Library of Congress   88-14561
                                                                  CIP

Published by
BRUNNER/MAZEL, INC.
19 Union Square
New York, New York 10003

MANUFACTURED IN THE UNITED STATES OF AMERICA

10 9 8 7 6 5 4 3 2

To my wife, Monica, and
my daughter, Elizabeth

Preface

For years it has been part of my job to train psychology graduate students to become useful members of treatment teams. The background that psychology students bring into the clinical setting is unusual: typically they have taken courses that give them a substantial theoretical knowledge, but they often have a limited amount of practical experience.

The practical know-how is a very important area of training; it is a basic requirement for being able to work effectively as a member of a multidisciplinary team. Professionals cannot collaborate well with one another if they do not have a system that is generally adhered to by all the members of the team. It is the knowledge of this system that allows one team member to understand the job that has been done by another member and in what way he or she can add to the evaluation or treatment that the client is receiving.

Entire books have been written about many of the areas covered by the present work. A more thorough review, however, would not share the information in a manner that is concise and practical enough to be of service to a person who has to perform a particular task without delay. This *Manual* evolved out of outlines I have written describing the different tasks that psychology students are called upon to do as part of their clinical work. With time, these lists became the chapters that follow.

The purpose of this *Manual* is to provide practical and easily understandable guidelines. This second edition contains the updates that have been made necessary by changes in the field since the publication of the first edition. For instance, the chapter on psychopathology now reflects the revision of the DSM-III, and new literature references have been included throughout the *Manual.* An effort has also been made to improve the value of the book to the trainee in other ways as well: the chapter on diagnostic methods was expanded and new sections have been added elsewhere, notably, those on the developmental and sociological perspectives.

By design, the coverage of particular areas will be simplistic. In some cases this simplistic approach will involve a certain naiveté, proposing one method as the way to accomplish an end and not doing justice to the many other ways in which the same goal may be reasonably accomplished. In other cases the simplification will involve offering only superficial information about a complex topic. As students progress, they will discover that our field is such that there is seldom only one way of doing anything; the limitation inherent in occasionally presenting only one method is, I hope, balanced by the advantage of giving the neophyte one method that will work.

In order to remedy the superficiality, readers should eventually acquaint themselves with other sources in order to acquire the deeper understanding that will be necessary. To help students choose books that will further their knowledge, references are given in the text. A full list is also included at the end of this volume. The books chosen are those that I personally have found helpful in training students.

James P. Choca, Ph.D.

Acknowledgments

This work contains the contributions of many individuals. Most obvious are the contributions of past and present members of the staff at the Lakeside Veterans Administration, especially Linda Bresolin, Michael Bresolin, Diane Cohen, Kay Cooper, John Gerber, James Daniels, Jonathon Goldman, Manuel Gonzales, Evelyn Graham, Jerry Grant, Mort Hammer, Walter Kitt, Elie Mangoubi, Althea Mason, Kun Ki Min, Jeri Morris, David Ostrow, Charles Peterson, Kathy Pietschman, Leonard Porter, Colleen Ryan, Jesus Sanchez, Lee Schwartz, Fred Stulp, Linda Topping, and Erich Van Denburg.

The support of the upper management at the V.A. Lakeside Medical Center, especially Dr. Irwin Singer and Mr. Joseph Moore, has been appreciated. I have also been influenced by my work as an attending psychologist in several private hospitals; in this area the work done with Dr. Rose Gomez has been especially valuable. What has been learned from the school personnel in the districts in which I am a diagnostic consultant is reflected in the school evaluation section of the *Manual.*

Dr. Elie Mangoubi and my father, Dr. Santiago Choca, were very helpful in revising the section on drug treatment. The section on neuropsychological testing was reviewed by Dr. Joseph Bleiberg. Dr. Luke Shanley helped with the section on family therapy. Drs. Theodore Millon, Robert Meagher, and Cathy Green must be thanked for the classification and development of the personality styles presented in this *Manual* and for the many years of research collaboration.

I am also grateful to all the psychology students who, while getting their training, helped to clarify what the important issues were and helped to develop ways of handling them.

James P. Choca, Ph.D.

Contents

Preface vii
Acknowledgments ix
List of Tables xiii

I. BASICS **1**
    A. Introduction 1
    B. Abilities 1
    C. Motivations 2
    D. Personality Style Theory 2
    E. Personality Styles 4
    F. Developmental Perspective 9
    G. Sociological Perspective 11

II. PSYCHOPATHOLOGY **15**
    A. Introduction 15
    B. Organic Mental Disorders 18
    C. Personality Disorders 21
    D. Clinical Syndromes in Adults 23
    E. Reactive Disorders 32
    F. Clinical Syndromes in Children and Adolescents 33

III. THE DIAGNOSTIC INTERVIEW **39**
    A. Introduction 39
    B. The Mental Status Examination 44
    C. A Diagnostic Interview 46
    D. A Report of a Psychological Evaluation 53

IV. PSYCHOLOGICAL TESTING **57**
    A. Introduction 57
    B. School Evaluations 59
    C. Intellectual Evaluation of Adults 68
    D. Testing for Psychodynamics 82
    E. Vocational Testing 106

V. PATIENT MANAGEMENT **113**
    A. The Problem-Oriented Approach 113
    B. Developing a Treatment Plan 113
    C. The Treatment Contract 119
    D. The Therapeutic Stance 120
    E. Handling Difficult Situations 121

VI. TREATMENT METHODS **125**
  A. Personality-Based Supportive Therapy 125
  B. Fundamentals of Individual Therapy 126
  C. Fundamentals of Group Therapy 128
  D. Fundamentals of Family Therapy 131
  E. Specific Therapeutic Techniques 133
  F. Fundamentals of Drug Treatment 139

VII. THE CLINICAL RECORD **149**
  A. Introduction 149

VIII. DISPOSITIONAL DECISIONS **161**
  A. Introduction 161
  B. The Referral Process 163
  C. Mental Health Settings 164

IX. PROFESSIONAL ISSUES **167**
  A. Ethical Principles 167
  B. Legal Issues 168
  C. Insurance 172

References 173

List of Tables

TABLE 1. Characteristics of the Millon Personality Styles 5
TABLE 2. Diagnostic Groups with Their Basic Etiology and Characteristics 17
TABLE 3. Organic Brain Syndromes 18
TABLE 4. Clinical Syndromes in Adults 24
TABLE 5. Disorders of Childhood and Adolescence 34
TABLE 6. School Diagnoses and Diagnostic Indicators 61
TABLE 7. Main Input Functions of the Brain 69
TABLE 8. Main Process Functions of the Brain 70
TABLE 9. Main Output Functions of the Brain 72
TABLE 10. Commonly Used Personality Inventories 83
TABLE 11. Commonly Used Projective Techniques 84
TABLE 12. Commonly Used Vocational Inventories 107
TABLE 13. Problems Commonly Seen in Psychiatric Patients ... 114
TABLE 14. Possible Therapeutic Plans 119
TABLE 15. Supportive Interventions for the Different Personality Styles 126
TABLE 16. Abbreviations Used in Medication Prescriptions 140
TABLE 17. Sedative Hypnotic Agents 141
TABLE 18. Minor Tranquilizers 142
TABLE 19. Neuroleptics 143
TABLE 20. Antidepressants 145
TABLE 21. Therapeutic Agents Used in Bipolar or Schizoaffective Disorders 147
TABLE 22. Antiparkinsonian Agents 148
TABLE 23. Abbreviations Often Used in Medical Records 153

I Basics

I.A. INTRODUCTION

To achieve a functional mental health perspective, professionals must take into account the entire system in which their client exists. The system is made up of (a) the individual, (b) the environment, and (c) the interaction between the two. Understanding the individual involves understanding his or her (a) abilities, (b) motivations, (c) personality structure, and (d) developmental stage in life.

The environment includes the racial, ethnic, and social aspects of the individual's family, job, and community. All parts of the system are intimately interrelated: the individual both influences and is influenced by the environment. Professionals guide their energies toward understanding or changing the individual, the environment, or both. Those who emphasize the former feel that the problems are often with the client and with his or her ability to adjust to the environment. It then makes the most sense to help the client overcome what would be perceived as his or her deficiency. An environmental approach argues either that environmental forces have precluded a viable adjustment or that the client has little ability to cope with the situation; in either case, this option proposes that changing the environment makes the most sense. Finally, the systemic viewpoint would hold that the problem is in the interaction of the different aspects of the system, including both the individual and the environment. This *Manual* will attempt to present all three areas of focus and will encourage the student to approach each client with an open mind. In other words, the professional should learn as much as possible about the client and his or her environment before deciding if the emphasis should be placed on the client, the environment, or both.

I.B. ABILITIES

Understanding the client's abilities becomes most important when such abilities are out of the ordinary. The assets and opportunities that are afforded to an individual who has outstanding abilities become an important part of his or her life. More often, however, clinicians have to help those who—for one reason or another—have significantly limited abilities compared to the majority of the population.

An ability below what is normally required to function is referred to as a disability, a deficit, or an impairment. The findings have generally been that

1

the milder the deficit, the longer the individual has had to struggle with it, and the younger the person was when the deficit was acquired, the easier the adjustment will be. A good adjustment usually involves a capacity to see oneself in a manner other than as a "handicapped" person while retaining a good appreciation for the abilities that are lacking (Schontz, 1982).

I.C. MOTIVATIONS

The conscious and unconscious goals that the person has at any particular time will determine to a great extent how the person will behave. As a result, many clinicians invest much time and effort in discovering and evaluating what the person's goals may be.

I.D. PERSONALITY STYLE THEORY

Another element that the individual brings into any situation is his or her personality. Although a person's behavior may change from one situation to another, the concept of personality style refers to attributes that tend to remain stable and that may be seen as the "essence" of that particular person.

The personality style is a cluster of personality traits that can be seen in individuals who are able to function well psychologically and that fit together as an integrated whole. Personality styles include:
  (a) A basic assumption about the self and the world that may or may not be at the conscious level.
  (b) Feelings about the self and the world, which are usually compatible with the basic assumptions.
  (c) Habitual behaviors, which are consistent with the basic assumptions and feelings. By far the most important behaviors are those that affect the interpersonal relationships of the individual.

Every personality style has advantages and disadvantages. For instance, the spontaneity and easy emotionality of the histrionic allow such a person to communicate feelings well but may make him or her overly dramatic and uninhibited. The effectiveness of a particular personality style partly depends on the situation that the person is facing: the assumption that life is a competitive situation where others may try to exploit us may be helpful when buying a used car but may be less useful when dealing with a spouse; the trait of orderliness gives the individual an edge when organizing a term paper but may cause the same person to be seen as a bit of a stuffed shirt in social situations.

According to personality style theory, the more adaptive individuals are those who:

(a) Have a definite personality style involving assumptions, feelings, and behaviors that are within some "normal" range.
(b) Are flexible and able to adjust to different situations. This flexibility involves being able to accept assumptions, have feelings, and produce behaviors that differ from the particular individual's usual tendency. Thus, for example, a well-adjusted individual who tends to be submissive and dependent needs to play a somewhat more dominant role in order to be successful when teaching a class.

A personality style can be a source of pathology if any of the following are true:
(a) The style is so disorganized or undeveloped that it does not serve to provide a routine way of relating to the world and/or a reasonable self-identity.
(b) The style contains incompatible assumptions, feelings, or behavior trends so that the individual is constantly struggling with a great amount of conflict.
(c) The style contains assumptions, feelings, or traits that are exaggerated to such a degree that they are no longer within a viable range.
(d) The individual adheres to the personality style so rigidly as to be unable to adjust to situations in which the particular personality style is not functional.

Most of the terms that will be used here to describe personality styles have a negative connotation. This is unfortunate, since the great majority of the population has a recognizable personality style and, in most cases, this cluster of personality traits serves the person well. Nevertheless, positive terms turn out to be much less revealing. For one thing, positive terms have less power in differentiating among people. (Most of us would admit to being "cooperative" but not to being "submissive" or "compliant.") Moreover, a term like "schizoid" or "compulsive" is much more meaningful to an experienced mental health professional than any substitute because it is the term used by the professional literature. Nevertheless, the terms in parentheses given in the next section represent reasonable alternatives.

The difference between personality disorders and personality styles should be emphasized. Most individuals have some assumptions about themselves and the world around which their personality styles may be defined. Only a few individuals have such problems with their assumptions or feelings that they are unable to function. Only the latter can be said to have a "personality disorder." The personality style of an individual does not imply the presence of psychopathology.

Personality styles are unique, and any classification of possible styles will—by necessity—do an injustice to the concept. When no system is attempted, however, it is very difficult for anyone but the most experienced clinician to use the concept productively. When formally classified, few individuals fit neatly into one of the personality categories. Most of us combine the basic styles in proportions that are unique to us. Thus, it is often advisable to take two or three of the individual's most prominent personality styles into consideration.

Since it is often difficult to conceptualize the different personality styles, the following literary works are offered. Each depicts a character with an approximation of the indicated personality style:

   (a) *Ward No. 6* by Anton Chekhov (avoidant)
   (b) *Oblomov* by Ivan Goncharov (dependent)
   (c) *Paul's Case* by Willa Cather (histrionic)
   (d) *The Eternal Husband* by Fyodor Dostoevsky and *My Last Dutchess,* a poem by Robert Browning (narcissistic)
   (e) *Defender of the Faith* by Philip Roth or *Les Liaisons Dangereuses* by Christo Hampton (antisocial)
   (f) *The Man in a Case* by Anton Chekhov (compulsive)
   (g) *Tobias Mindernickel* by Thomas Mann (explosive)

I.E. PERSONALITY STYLES

Figure 1 maps out the scheme to be followed. The descriptions given here were adapted from those of Theodore Millon (1969). Table 1 gives a summary of the eight styles.

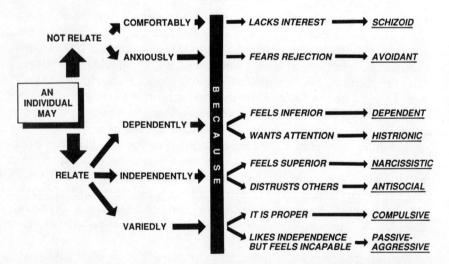

Figure 1. Basic Scheme for the Classification of Personality Styles.
(Adapted from T. Millon, *Modern Psychopathology.* Philadelphia: Saunders, 1969.)

TABLE 1. Characteristics of the Millon Personality Styles

Personality Style	Cognitive Characteristics	Emotional Characteristics	Interpersonal Characteristics
1. Schizoid	Lack of ability and interest in communicating with and understanding others	Unemotional, apathetic, indifferent	Lacks friends; relates in a distant manner
2. Avoidant	Values acceptance; fears rejection	Apprehensive, uneasy, anxious, nervous	Lacks friends; relates in a tentative manner and is likely to pull away
3. Dependent	Sees self as inferior, less capable or valuable than others	Unassuming	Cooperative, submissive, or dependent; tries to please others
4. Histrionic	Life becomes boring without frequent stimulation	Dramatic, emotional	Seeks attention; has temporary but involved relationships
5. Narcissistic	Sees self as superior, more capable or valuable than others	Proud, expansive	Assertive and dominant; seeks others who follow his/her lead
6. Antisocial	Views life as a competition; fears being taken advantage of	Cold, unemotional	Self-reliant; distrusting of others; tends to use others
7. Compulsive	Values perfection; fears making mistakes	Controlled, formal, proper	Compliant with those above; domineering and controlling to those below
8. Passive-aggressive; explosive	Sees self as needing others but does not see others as superior	Emotional fluctuations with frequent changes in mood	May be cooperative and friendly but then becomes resentful or hostile

1. The schizoid (introversive) style: Schizoid individuals are characterized by a relatively unemotional existence. When things turn out well, they do not seem particularly happy, but they are not too saddened by misfortune. They tend to be quiet, staying often by themselves and taking the role of passive observers. They remain uninvolved, very seldom taking sides or a strong position. Rarely the center of attention, these individuals often fade into the social background. They have a small number of friends and their relationships are without deep commitments. They do not fear or actively avoid people, but they are somewhat indifferent and apparently have little need to communicate or to obtain support from others. These individuals are unlikely to be passionate or lose control of their behavior, even in the most emotional situations. As a result, they may be seen as good judges or crisis workers; they may be good at any job that calls for the ability to remain detached, uninvolved, and objective. Schizoid people are often viewed, however, as somewhat dull, quiet and colorless, indifferent, and apathetic.

2. The avoidant (sensitive) style: Both the schizoid and the avoidant styles are similar in that they characterize people who lack interpersonal involvement in their everyday lives. In both cases, these individuals do not have close friends, tending to remain detached and isolated. In contrast to the unemotional schizoids, however, the avoidant individuals feel apprehensive when relating to others. They are usually shy and nervous in social situations. Strongly wishing to be liked and accepted by others, they fear rejection. Their concern with this rejection tends to put them on guard and make them uncomfortable. Social gatherings and other interpersonal situations are experienced with distaste. Relating to others is a difficult task which they often try to avoid. In so doing, however, they give up the support and affection that the avoided relationship could have brought. These individuals are sensitive, compassionate, and emotionally responsive. On the other hand, they are often nervous and awkward in social situations, mistrustful of other people, lonely, and isolated.

3. The dependent (cooperative) style: The life assumption of dependent individuals is that they are incapable of taking care of themselves and must find someone who is benevolent and dependable and who will support them emotionally. Individuals with this personality style have a tendency to form strong attachments to people who then take a dominant role in decision making. They are followers rather than leaders, taking a passive role in interpersonal affairs. They shy away from highly competitive situations. Concerned with losing friends, they cover up their true feelings, especially when the feelings are aggressive or objectionable. They are unconceited individuals who try to be as congenial as possible to

the people around them. These people are usually well liked, but they are sometimes considered wishy-washy because they never take a strong position on controversial issues. They can also be criticized for their tendency toward submissive dependency, for their lack of self-esteem, and for always looking outside themselves for help.

4. The histrionic (dramatic) style: Histrionics are colorful and overemotional individuals. They are people who seek stimulation, excitement, and attention. They react very readily to situations around them, often becoming very involved, but typically the involvement does not last. This pattern of getting involved and then becoming bored is repeated time after time. Histrionic people are very good at making positive first impressions. Their ability to react to unexpected situations, their alertness and interest, and their search for attention make them colorful and charming at parties and other social gatherings. Often, however, they can become too loud, exhibitionistic, and overly dramatic. They can be demanding and uncontrollable, especially when they are highly involved. They may have intense emotional moments in friendships, but their friendships are often short-lived and replaced when boredom sets in. Their dependency has a very different flavor from that of the dependent individual in that they need the attention of others rather than emotional support. As a result, they may be less submissive than dependent individuals.

5. The narcissistic (confident) style: The predominant assumption of narcissistic persons is that they are more competent and gifted than the rest of the people around them. This assumption gives them a flavor of mild grandiosity that colors their relationships. Usually the dominant figures in friendships, these people seek people who support their narcissistic needs. They may relate to others in a condescending and patronizing manner. They are sociable and independent individuals who feel good about themselves. They are not unduly influenced by the opinions of others and are capable of making their own decisions. They are often outspoken and colorful members of society. Possibly they can be criticized for being arrogant and presumptuous. They may be inconsiderate and exploitive of others, since they tend to feel that they are something special.

6. The antisocial (competitive) style: The world view of antisocial individuals is that of a "rat race." The assumption is that everyone is after the same things (money, fame, sexual enjoyment, etc.). The only way to get one's share is to be one step ahead of the crowd. Antisocial people are self-reliant, assertive, or even domineering and hostile. They are proud of this self-reliance and see themselves as "hard-headed realists." They view the world as cruel, a jungle where "might makes right." Warmth, gentleness, and compassion are often seen as ineffective signs of weakness, which

they avoid by being hard, cold, and aggressive. Their relationships with people are often superficial and chosen for material benefits. Friendships may be terminated when their usefulness ends. Because of their realistic outlook and emphasis on concrete gains, these people may be very good in business. On the positive side, they are competitive, realistic individuals who get things done. On the negative side, however, they may be cold, domineering, and insensitive, may be seen as afraid of their own feelings of warmth, and may be unable to trust others.

7. The compulsive (disciplined) style: The lifestyle of compulsive individuals is based on the premise that it would be terrible to make a mistake. Compulsive individuals are orderly and plan for the future. They are conscientious, usually well prepared, and try to get the work done on schedule. They are efficient, dependable, industrious, and persistent. To those in authority, they tend to relate in an overly respectful, ingratiating, and dependent manner. This style of relating often changes in the relationship with a subordinate, where they are prone to be arrogant and perfectionistic, treating the subordinate with disdain. Often these individuals believe in rules and practice self-restraint, especially when it concerns their own emotions, which they attempt to keep under control. The overcontrol of the emotions also tends to give compulsive individuals a characteristic flavor: they are often much too formal and proper and are unlikely to open up or act spontaneously in front of others. They are sometimes seen as perfectionistic, rigid, picayune, afraid of making a mistake, and indecisive before they have a chance to study all aspects of a problem.

8. The passive-aggressive or explosive (conflictual) style: This style is derived from two assumptions about the world that do not fit together well. The first assumption these people make is that they need to depend on others because they are not able to survive without support or attention. In this way, they are similar to the dependent or histrionic types. The contrast is created by the second premise, which is that they cannot afford to depend on others. These people often feel that others are not interested enough to be dependable or that dependence on others is not socially acceptable and will make them look bad. These assumptions may result in two different substyles. Passive-aggressive individuals handle the conflict by appearing cooperative on the surface but boycotting the efforts of others along the way. Explosive individuals vacillate between feeling that they are lucky and get more than they have a right to expect and feeling that the world has mistreated or cheated them. Their behavior changes accordingly. At times these people treat others in an agreeable and friendly manner; on other occasions they are irritable, aggressive, and hostile; at still

other times, they may be full of contrition and guilt. At times they are very optimistic and see the future as bright, but this changes, seemingly without reason, into the opposite view. In their work they also vacillate: an energetic and productive mood together with high goals characterizes them in some instances, but later they lower their goals and become less productive. These people are very flexible and changeable, sensitive and responsive to their environment, but they are also seen as moody and unpredictable.

I.F   DEVELOPMENTAL PERSPECTIVE

It is clear that life has a course with a beginning, a middle, and an end. The place in which an individual is along this course dictates to a significant extent the kind of task that the person is facing and the kind of resources that she or he will have available in facing that task.

The concept of "stages" of life is very prevalent in the thinking of developmental theorists. This concept not only involves the idea that there are different phases in life, but emphasizes the belief that any phase builds upon the previous ones. In the same way that a person cannot learn how to divide without first knowing how to subtract, forming adult relationships outside of the family of origin is problematic for a person who never had acceptable relationships at home. When understood in this manner, the concept of stages is a very powerful one. For instance, it means that in diagnosing a client's psychopathology, the psychologist should attempt to determine at what stage along the way the individual failed to meet the task of that phase of life. The person's poor performance in the stages that follow can then be understood in terms of the lack of the required preparation for that stage. The concept speaks in favor of using therapy to attempt to correct the deficits created by the unsuccessful completion of a previous stage in life.

In some ways the concept of stages is a deterministic way of thinking about human development: if a correction of the developmental problem is not possible or has not been accomplished, the individual is forever doomed to a poor level of performance. The concept explains very nicely how, after great musical accomplishments as a child, Beethoven went on to become the musical genius he became; it has more difficulty explaining the success of many others (including Albert Einstein) who did not have such outstanding early achievements in the area in which they became eminent figures. Although it can be argued in such cases that there was a "corrective" experience along the way, it seems also reasonable to assume that an individual's abilities, motivations, and personality may be much more helpful in one phase of life than in another. The child with a mildly elevated energy level may have difficulty sitting in the classroom but may later become the hard-driving founder and president of a computer manufacturing company; the shy adolescent may have significant difficulties finding a wife during early adulthood but may become a very well adjusted husband when the demands for social abilities have lessened.

In other words, it may be helpful to the psychologist to understand both how early failures can contribute to continued difficulties later on, and the elements that can be advantageous or disadvantageous at one stage of life and not at others. With either point of view, however, the psychologist has to be acquainted with the life task that the client is facing in order to be able to use a developmental perspective. A summary of the generally accepted stages and the tasks associated with that phase of life follows.

1. Childhood: ages 0 to 12. This period involves the development of perceptual, motoric, and thinking abilities and the gradual construction of a separate identity. The realization that others have a unique self and the issues of attachment and differentiation are probably the most important psychological tasks of early childhood. The social role is eventually expanded further to include relationships outside of the home.

2. Adolescence: ages 12 to 20. Puberty marks the entrance into adolescence. The sexual maturity that develops during this period necessitates dealing with gender relationships in a very different way than before. Confusion and preoccupation with sexual issues may become prevalent. Especially toward the end of this period, the task of separating from the family of origin becomes a dominant force. This task may be partially accomplished through a certain amount of rebelliousness and conflict with authority figures. While this is happening, peer relationships and peer opinions become much more important than in probably any other period of life.

3. Early adulthood: ages 17 to 45. This period is marked by the peak of biological functioning of the individual. Formal schooling has ended or will typically end at the beginning of adulthood. The individual has to set up what Levinson (1978) calls the first "life structure" by acquiring his or her own family and developing an occupation. The first major choices have to be made. More often than not, these choices involve compromise and the abandonment of some goals in order to achieve others. Having made the choices, the person becomes a "novice," often to be "mentored" by an older co-worker or supervisor. This life structure is reviewed at different times during adulthood. The fact that the person is evaluating his or her life structure may or may not be obvious to the individual. Sometimes these reviews are the source of much psychological pain and mark the onset of psychopathology. At times these self-evaluations may

lead to drastic life changes, such as a change of sexual orientation, a divorce, or a change of occupation. In other instances, the life structure may emerge fairly intact. By the end of this period, the person should have established a niche in society; she or he should have "settled down" into a defined role, family, circle of friends, and so on.

4. Midlife: ages 40 to 65. The period of middle adulthood typically involves the issue of becoming a senior member of society. Struggling with this issue of aging, the person has gradually moved from being the junior member of the staff at work to eventually becoming an authority figure. The responsibility for the care of children in the home replicates this line of development in the person's personal life. As the period evolves further, the competitiveness of one's youth is replaced by compassion and an appreciation for family relationships in the case of men. There are also indications that the opposite trend takes place with women. In their case, as midlife comes to a close, the person becomes more interested in the world that exists outside of the home and becomes more aggressive or competitive.

5. Late adulthood: ages 60 and older. This period is marked by retirement and the gradual but eventual deterioration of the organism. The reduced occupational and family responsibilities are experienced partly as a relief, as an opportunity to free oneself from a burden and do whatever it was that could not be done in one's life prior to this time. In some ways, however, these changes represent a threat, a loss in importance in society, a loss of that niche that was so carefully created in early adulthood and nurtured through the middle years. The presence of medical problems and reduced physical capacity and stamina eventually force the individual to struggle with the issue of death and whatever legacy one is able to leave behind.

Further information about childhood and adolescence can be obtained from any developmental psychology textbook. The work of Levinson (1978) or Vaillant (1977) is highly recommended for a deeper understanding of adulthood. Neugarten (1968) is a good reference for information on the older adult.

I.G. SOCIOLOGICAL PERSPECTIVE

The importance of cultural, socioeconomic, educational, and gender differences has been known for many years. These factors affect the clinician's ability to establish rapport with the client and to understand the client accurately.

Working with professionals of different sexes, races, and cultural backgrounds, one finds that clients tend to gravitate toward "their own kind." This is not to say that professionals can only work with individuals who are similar to themselves, but that social issues have to be taken into account when choosing or assigning clients, especially when the client's own personality style or psychopathology will make the establishment of the therapeutic alliance problematic.

Most of the psychological literature addressing social differences deals with the issue of understanding the client. There are, for instance, many anecdotal accounts of misperceptions of the client during evaluations or therapy. More scientific studies have been able to show cultural differences in the way persons from different cultural backgrounds look at the concept of time, the concept of aging, the relationships in the family.

Psychological studies have been able to show, moreover, that individuals from different cultural backgrounds can be expected to perform differently on psychological tests. Generally, the studies have demonstrated that the average for American Blacks or Hispanic Americans may be as much as ten points lower than for the average for White Americans in standardized intelligence tests. These findings have led to a great controversy surrounding the issue of whether the tests are valid and measure real differences between the cultures or are "biased" and make the members of a particular minority look worse than the majority culture. The legal battles that have ensued have not been able to provide much guidance. The suit by the Golden Rule Insurance Company against Educational Testing Service was settled out of court, but the settlement is still hotly debated (Anrig, 1987). The battle against the California school system resulted in a ban on using the tests as the main instrument to place Blacks in educable mentally handicapped (EMH) special education rooms (Lambert, 1981; *Larry P.* v. *Riles,* 1979), but a similar battle in Chicago led to a decision in favor of the psychological tests (*PASE* v. *Hannon,* 1980).

Psychological tests are arguably the most objective and valid way of assessing a client. Perhaps the main reason the racial controversy has surrounded testing rather than clinical assessments made on the basis of other sources of information is that scores provide a clear indication of the assessment that would be made about the client. The prevalence of prejudicial judgments against members of a minority culture that are based on the intangibles of what goes on during a diagnostic interview, for instance, cannot even be guessed at. The lesson to learn is that we must be as aware as possible of any cultural differences that may exist in the case of a particular client; the issue often is how the client is different from the well-functioning members of his cultural group rather than how the client differs from us.

Further information can be obtained from:

Brisbane, F. L., & Womble, M. (Eds.). (1985). *Treatment of Black alcoholics.* New York: Haworth Press.

Brodsky, A. M., & Hare-Mustin, R. (Eds.). (1980). *Women and psychotherapy.* New York: Guilford Press.

Gender issues in psychotherapy. (1986). *Psychotherapy, 23*(2).

Jensen, A. R. (1980). *Bias in mental testing.* New York: Free Press.

Martinez, J. L., & Mendoza, R. H. (Eds.). (1984). *Chicano psychology* (2nd ed.). Orlando, FL: Academic Press.

McGoldrick, M., Pearce, J. K., & Giordano, J. (Eds.). (1982). *Ethnicity and family therapy.* New York: Guilford Press.

Turner, S. M., & Jones, R. T. (1982). *Behavior modification in Black populations: Psychosocial issues and empirical findings.* New York: Plenum Publishing Co.

Watts, T. D., & Wright, R., Jr. (1983). *Black alcoholism: Towards a comprehensive understanding.* Springfield, IL: Charles C Thomas.

II Psychopathology

II.A. INTRODUCTION

As the individual's abilities, motivation, and personality style interact with the environment, a certain amount of friction or emotional stress may develop. The amount of friction that is comfortable or tolerable differs from one person to another. Also, situations that are troublesome or raise the stress felt by one individual may not be problematic at all for another. As long as the amount of friction is kept below the tolerated threshold, no pathology will emerge. When this is not the case and the individual is not able to reduce the stress, psychopathology may result, as shown in Figure 2. As the diagram shows, pathological behavior often increases the amount of friction that the individual has with the environment. Psychopathology is often seen as having a dual role—it can be both the cause and the effect of excessive friction with the environment.

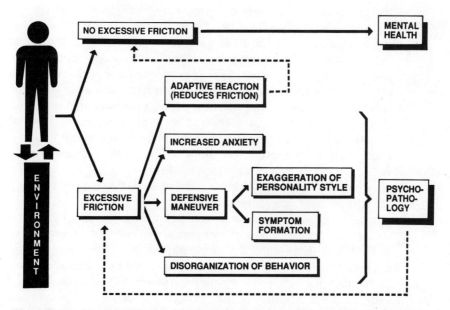

Figure 2. The Possible Effects of the Individual's Interactions with the Environment.

If we define psychopathology as dysfunctional behavior, we can discriminate among three different types:

(a) *Organic pathology*—where there is something biologically wrong with the individual's functioning, so that the person does not have the ability to behave in ways that would accomplish his or her goal because of a misfunctioning of the brain itself;

(b) *Functional pathology*—where the individual, for psychological reasons, chooses to behave in ways that do not accomplish his or her goals effectively;

(c) *Situational pathology*—where there is something so stressful about the situation confronting the person that there is little or nothing that can be done in order to accomplish the person's goals. Although many clear cases of organic, functional, or situational pathologies are found, there are also a great number of cases that fall into a gray area. The assessment of depression in a demented patient, organicity in schizophrenics, or premorbid emotional problems in individuals with a post-traumatic stress disorder is obviously very difficult, in spite of the great amount of research that has been already invested in these areas. The issue is compounded by the fact that there are mental health professionals who favor one etiological explanation over the others and would argue, for instance, that most schizophrenics or depressed individuals in reality suffer from an organic disorder, perhaps a yet to be discovered chemical imbalance.

Functional pathology can be of two types:

(a) An exaggeration of the basic personality style. For example, an individual with a disciplined personality style may be uncomfortable with developments at work. Feeling threatened, the person makes an effort to increase the control he or she exerts on the environment, a typical compulsive strategy. Such a person may insist that others do things his or her way, may become more preoccupied with trivial details, and so on. As with this example, many of the psychopathological symptoms that result from exaggerations of the personality style would fall in the area of a personality disorder.

(b) A symptom formation or addition of symptoms that may be compatible with, but are different from, the basic personality style. A state of panic, the need to wash hands constantly, somatic complaints, and depression are examples of symptoms that may be present in an individual with a compulsive personality style.

Table 2 lists the different diagnostic groups with their main characteristics. The classification of psychopathology by the American Psychiatric Association presented in the revision of the third edition of the *Diagnostic and Statistical Manual of Mental Disorders* (DSM-III-R, 1987) requires the coding of data into five axes, as follows:

Axis I—Clinical syndromes (see sections B, D, E, and F of this chapter)

Axis II—Personality disorder (see section C), if present; otherwise, personality style (see Chapter I)

Axis III—Physical disorder potentially relevant to understanding or managing an emotional problem

Axis IV—Severity of psychosocial stressors

Axis V—Highest level of adaptive functioning during the past year

The severity of the psychosocial stressor is coded in a scale from 0 to 6, with 0 being information not available, 1 signifying that no psychosocial stressors were present during the last year, and 6 indicating that catastrophic stressors had occurred. The highest level of functioning during the last year is rated on a scale from 1 to 100, with 100 indicating optimal functioning, 60 signifying that moderate symptoms were present, and 1 reflecting an inability to take care of even basic functions like personal hygiene.

Every diagnostic group includes a category called "not otherwise specified" or "NOS" (e.g., organic mental syndrome, not otherwise specified). This label is used for individuals who show disorders that fit in that diagnostic group (e.g., an organic mental syndrome) but who do not meet the criteria for any of the specific disorders.

The DSM-III-R also recognizes "conditions" that are not classified as mental disorders but that can be the focus of attention and treatment. These conditions include: academic problems, adult antisocial behaviors, borderline intellectual functioning, childhood or adolescent antisocial behaviors, malingering, marital problems, noncompliance with medical treatment, occupational problems, parent-child problems, other interpersonal problems, other specified family circumstances, phase of life problems, and uncomplicated bereavement. All of these conditions are noted on Axis I with the exception of borderline intellectual functioning.

TABLE 2. Diagnostic Groups with Their Basic Etiology and Characteristics

Main Problem Area	Diagnostic Group	Main Characteristic
Brain functioning	Organic mental disorders	
Psychological functioning	Personality disorders	Exaggeration of basic personality style
	Clinical syndromes in adults	Symptoms added on to the basic personality style
Environmental stress	Reactive disorders	Symptoms precipitated by the occurrence of a traumatic situation
_____	Clinical syndromes in childhood and adolescence	Disorders that arise in childhood or adolescence

II.B.   ORGANIC MENTAL DISORDERS

If we use a computer model, we can say that an organic mental disorder represents a malfunctioning of the machinery itself. In these cases, individuals do not function properly because their ability to perceive, understand, or act upon a particular situation is neurologically impaired.

The syndromes that make up the organic mental disorders (or organic brain syndromes) can be grouped into eleven different clusters, as shown in Table 3. Often there are difficult diagnostic issues involved with the organic brain syndromes. First, the presence of the disorder has to be established. For this task, the mental status examination (see section III.B) can be used as a rough screening device. Any questionable findings should be documented further with neuropsychological testing (see section IV.C). Finally, a neurological exam should be obtained through consultation with a neurologist.

After the presence of an organic syndrome has been established, it is often necessary to rule out the existence of other disorders. This task is often hard, because many neurological impairments present clinical pictures that resemble emotional syndromes. A good clinical history and evaluation are the tools used to accomplish this task. If the clinical picture coincides with any of the functional disorders, it is necessary to document that the behav-

TABLE 3. Organic Brain Syndromes

No.	Group	Main Characteristic
1	Delirium	Disturbance of attention and thought control
2	Dementia	Intellectual impairment
3	Amnestic syndrome	Memory impairment
4	Organic delusional syndrome	Presence of delusions
5	Organic hallucinatory syndrome	Presence of hallucinations
6	Organic mood syndrome	Mood instability
7	Organic anxiety syndrome	Anxiety or panic attacks
8	Organic personality syndrome	Disturbance of temperament or emotional dysfunction
9	Intoxication	Disturbance of intellectual and motor functioning due to substance use
10	Withdrawal	Disturbance of intellectual and motor functioning due to withdrawal of substance from the system
11	Organic mental syndrome NOS	Does not meet criteria for any of the above

iors in question were present before the onset of the organicity. If this is not the case, it may be assumed that the personality change was the direct or indirect result of the organicity.

The mental retardations are usually the result of neurological damage. However, under the present system, they are considered disorders of childhood and adolescence rather than organic brain syndromes.

The organic brain syndromes may be temporary or permanent, depending on their etiology. Further information regarding specific neurological disorders can be obtained by consulting any neurological textbook, such as Curtis, Jacobson, and Marcus (1972) or Patton, Sundsten, Crill, and Swanson (1976).

The diagnosis of any of the following can be made only when there is evidence that the symptoms result from organic pathology:

1. *Delirium:* A delirium is a disturbance of attention accompanied by disorganized rambling and irrelevant or incoherent thinking. It is usually also accompanied by disorientation, a reduced level of consciousness, a sleep disorder, changes in psychomotor activity, or perceptual misinterpretations. When the delirium is related to substance abuse, one of the terms that follow should be used:
   (a) Alcohol withdrawal delirium (delirium tremens)—takes place in an individual who stops alcohol ingestion after a period of heavy drinking. It is usually accompanied by tachycardia, sweating, and elevated blood pressure.
   (b) Sedative, hypnotic, or anxiolytic withdrawal delirium—same as the alcohol withdrawal delirium.
   (c) Phencyclidine (PCP) or similarly acting drug delirium—follows intake of such drug.
   (d) Amphetamine or similar substance delirium—follows intake of such a toxic substance.
   (e) Cocaine delirium.

2. *Dementia:* A dementia is a deterioration of both short- and long-term memory, together with an impairment of judgment and abstract thinking ability, usually accompanied by other organic indicators such as aphasia (language dysfunction), apraxia (inability to carry out motor movements), constructional difficulty (inability to reproduce figures), or a personality change. Dementias can be seen together with delirium, delusions, or depression and have a senile (after age 65) or presenile onset. When appropriate, one of the specific terms that follow should be used:
   (a) *Primary degenerative dementia*—a progressive dementia of the Alzheimer type.

(b) *Multi-infarct dementia*—involves the deterioration of some intellectual functions but not of others and is accompanied by focal neurological signs. This dementia is caused by multiple cerebral infarcts, often secondary to chronic hypertension.

(c) *Alcohol or substance abuse dementia*—occurs in an individual who has abused alcohol or another substance for a prolonged period of time and persists even after the individual is well detoxified.

3. *Amnestic syndrome:* An amnestic syndrome is a disturbance of both short-term and long-term memory functions in which attention, judgment, and abstract thinking remain unimpaired. When the syndrome is connected to substance abuse, the correct diagnosis would be alcohol, sedative, hypnotic, anxiolytic, or other substance amnestic syndrome.

4. *Organic delusional syndrome:* Involves the presence of false beliefs. A delusional syndrome may be an amphetamine, hallucinogen, cannabis, cocaine, PCP, or other substance delusional syndrome if it develops as a result of recent drug intake.

5. *Organic hallucinatory syndrome:* Involves a false perception occurring with alertness and in the absence of other intellectual deficits. It may be an alcohol, hallucinogen, or other substance hallucinatory syndrome if it develops as a result of recent drug intake. There is also a post-hallucinogen perception disorder which involves the reexperiencing of the perceptual symptoms, or "flashback," after the person is no longer intoxicated.

6. *Organic mood syndrome:* Involves a prominent and persistent manic or depressive state. When appropriate, the diagnosis of PCP, hallucinogen, or other substance abuse mood syndrome should be used.

7. *Organic anxiety syndrome:* Prominent and recurrent panic attacks or generalized anxiety.

8. *Organic personality syndrome:* Disorder involving fluctuations of mood, impulsiveness, irritability, impairment of social judgment, apathy, or suspiciousness.

9. *Intoxication:* Intoxications are maladaptive behaviors that result from the recent intake of specific drugs. They are classified according to the drug used as follows:
   (a) *Alcohol intoxication*
   (b) *Alcohol idiosyncratic intoxication (when only a small amount of alcohol produces the toxic state)*
   (c) *Sedative, hypnotic, or anxiolytic intoxication*

(d) *Opioid intoxication*

(e) *Cannabis (marijuana) intoxication*

(f) *Cocaine intoxication*

(g) *Amphetamine intoxication*

(h) *Caffeine intoxication*

(i) *Inhalant intoxication*

(j) *Phencyclidine (PCP) or similarly acting drug intoxication*

(k) *Other substance intoxication*

The specific symptoms expected depend on the type of drug used.

10. *Drug withdrawal:* Some drugs cause a physical dependence so that, when an individual takes the drug for a period of time and then stops, a number of physical symptoms may result. Withdrawals are classified according to the drug used as follows:

(a) *Alcohol withdrawal*—this diagnosis is used only when delirium tremens is not present (see #1 above)

(b) *Sedative, hypnotic, or anxiolytic withdrawal*

(c) *Opioid withdrawal*

(d) *Amphetamine withdrawal*

(e) *Cocaine withdrawal*

(f) *Nicotine withdrawal*

(g) *Other substance withdrawal*

As above, the specific symptoms expected depend on the type of drug use.

11. *Organic mental syndrome not otherwise specified* (NOS).

II.C. PERSONALITY DISORDERS

The personality disorders or character disorders consist of a lifelong pattern of behavior that is maladaptive enough to present significant problems in terms of the individual's functioning. These disorders are often exaggerations of the individual's basic personality style. In fact, many of the syndromes differ from the Millon personality styles (presented in Chapter I) only in the magnitude of the personality traits.

The paranoid, schizotypal, and borderline personality disorders do not have a Millon personality style equivalent. Nevertheless, they are often exaggerations of the personality style of the individual. For instance, the paranoid personality disorder is often related to antisocial or passive-aggressive traits.

There are several disorders of childhood and adolescence that are rough equivalents of personality disorders (e.g., the introverted disorder of childhood, the shyness disorder, the conduct disorder, the oppositional disorder, and the identity disorder). These, however, will be covered in section F, describing the clinical syndromes in children and adolescents.

The disorders that follow will be presented in the order used in Chapter I. However, the DSM-III-R presents them in three clusters, as follows:

A. Odd or eccentric   (Paranoid, schizoid, schizotypal)
B. Dramatic, emotional,   (Antisocial, borderline, histrionic, narcissistic)
   or erratic
C. Anxious or fearful   (Avoidant, dependent, obsessive-compulsive,
                          passive-aggressive)

A requirement for all personality disorders is the presence of a pervasive and unwarranted tendency in a variety of different situations that represents a lifelong maladaptive lifestyle. Personality disorders cannot be diagnosed prior to early adulthood.

1. *Schizoid personality disorder:* Disorder characterized by withdrawal and isolation with few close friendships. These individuals lack the capacity and interest to relate to others, are indifferent to praise and criticism, and appear apathetic and unemotional.

2. *Avoidant personality disorder:* Disorder characterized by a fear of and hypersensitivity to rejection by others, timidity and social discomfort, with a resulting reluctance to establish close friendships in a person who desires to be liked and accepted.

3. *Dependent personality disorder:* Disorder characterized by a pattern of submissive and dependent behaviors in an individual who lacks self-confidence and who is uncomfortable when alone or unsupported.

4. *Histrionic personality disorder:* Disorder characterized by a pattern of dramatic, overly emotional behaviors together with seductiveness, superficiality, demandingness, egocentrism, dependency, or helplessness.

5. *Narcissistic personality disorder:* Disorder characterized by a pattern of grandiose and exhibitionistic behaviors, inability to accept criticism, a tendency to expect that others will be submissive and attentive, and a lack of empathy for others.

6. *Antisocial personality disorder:* Disorder characterized by criminal activities, rebelliousness, substance abuse, lying, irresponsibility, interpersonal exploitiveness, and interpersonal or occupational instability in an individual who is not schizophrenic or manic. For the diagnosis to be used, evidence of a conduct disorder present before age 15 is required.

7. *Obsessive-compulsive personality disorder:* Disorder characterized by perfectionism, scrupulousness, a preoccupation with trivial details, discomfort when the person is not in control, rigidity and inability to make decisions expediently, difficulty in expressing tenderness, and excessive devotion to work.

8. *Passive-aggressive personality disorder:* Disorder characterized by a resentful, obstructionistic, or negativistic attitude so that the individual is superficially compliant but demonstrates resistance through procrastination, intentional inefficiency, and irritability or argumentativeness.

9. *Schizotypal personality disorder:* Disorder characterized by eccentricity and withdrawal without other psychotic symptoms. These behaviors may include superstitiousness, odd beliefs, ideas of reference, tangentiality or circumstantiality, inappropriate emotional responses, suspiciousness, excessive social anxiety, and the lack of close friends.

10. *Paranoid personality disorder:* Disorder characterized by a tendency to misconstrue normal actions as hostile or threatening, a distrust of others, an inclination to bear grudges, and a hypersensitivity to real or imagined criticisms.

11. *Borderline personality disorder:* Disorder characterized by instability of mood, self-image, and interpersonal relationships. It may also include impulsivity in potentially self-damaging areas, inappropriate intense anger, recurrent suicidal threats, chronic feelings of meaninglessness, and discomfort when alone.

12. *Personality disorders not otherwise specified.*

II.D.   CLINICAL SYNDROMES IN ADULTS

Exaggerations of the basic personality style can, in some cases, be part of the disorders presented in this section. For example, the obsessive-compulsive anxiety disorder may involve repeated hand washing, which can be seen as an extreme example of the cleanliness of a compulsive personality style. Most typically, however, these syndromes represent pathology that is added on to the basic personality style.

Although most of the symptoms covered in this section do not result directly from the basic personality style, the individual's style remains an important factor. For instance, a paranoid schizophrenic disorder in a compulsive individual is often colored by a rigidity, a righteousness, or a perfectionism that is an obvious reminder of the basic character structure. In comparison, the same disorder in a narcissistic individual is typically flavored by grandiosity and feelings of omnipotence.

Table 4 shows the basic classification scheme. A description of the different disorders can be found on the following pages.

TABLE 4. Clinical Syndromes in Adults

No.	Disorder Group	Basic Characteristic
	Drug-Related Disorders	
1	Psychoactive substance abuse	Impairment of functioning
2	Psychoactive substance dependence	Physical dependence
	Psychoses	
3	Schizophrenic disorders	Disorganization of the thinking process
4	Delusional disorders	Persecutory delusions or delusions of jealousy without disorganization of the thinking process
5	Other psychoses	Atypical and mixed psychotic disorders
	Neuroses	
6	Mood disorders	Changes in mood
7	Anxiety disorders	Anxiety, panic states, or irrational fears
8	Factitious disorders	Production of symptoms under voluntary control
9	Somatoform disorders	Physical complaints without organic causes and not under voluntary control
10	Dissociative disorders	Disorders of consciousness
	Sexual Disorders	
11	Paraphilias	Sexual arousal produced by unusual sexual objects
12	Sexual dysfunctions	Inability to function adequately sexually
	Sleep Disorders	
13	Dyssomnias	Disturbance of the period of time the person sleeps
14	Parasomnias	Disturbance occurring while the person is asleep
	Other Disorders	
15	Impulse control disorders	Failure to resist harmful impulses

All of the clinical syndromes are "functional disorders": these categories are to be used only when the behavior in question is thought not to be the result of an organic brain condition.

1. *Psychoactive substance abuse disorders:* The psychoactive substance abuse disorders involve an impairment of social, occupational, psychological, or physical functioning resulting from frequent and continued use of a particular drug. These disorders are classified according to the drug that is abused, as follows:
   (a) *Alcohol abuse disorder*
   (b) *Cannabis (marijuana) abuse disorder*
   (c) *Hallucinogen abuse disorder*
   (d) *Inhalant abuse disorder*
   (e) *Opioid abuse disorder*
   (f) *Cocaine abuse disorder*
   (g) *Amphetamine abuse disorder*
   (h) *Phencyclidine (PCP) or similarly acting drug abuse disorder*
   (i) *Sedative, hypnotic, or anxiolytic abuse disorder*
   (j) *Psychoactive substance abuse not otherwise specified*

2. *Psychoactive substance dependence disorders:* "Dependency" involves a physical need for the drug, characterized by the necessity of increasing the amount consumed in order to obtain the desired experience, a persistent desire for the drug, and social or occupational dysfunction. Physical withdrawal symptoms would follow the discontinuation of the drug. These disorders are classified by the type of drug used, as follows:
   (a) *Alcohol dependence*
   (b) *Cannabis (marijuana) dependence*
   (c) *Hallucinogen dependence*
   (d) *Opioid dependence*
   (e) *Cocaine dependence*
   (f) *Amphetamine dependence*
   (g) *Inhalant dependence*
   (h) *Nicotine dependence*
   (i) *Phencyclidine (PCP) or similarly acting drug dependence*
   (j) *Sedative, hypnotic, or anxiolytic dependence*
   (k) *Polysubstance dependence*
   (l) *Psychoactive substance dependence not otherwise specified*

3. *Schizophrenic disorders:* Schizophrenic disorders are characterized by a pervasive disturbance of the thought process severe enough to cause a significant impairment in the individual's ability to work, maintain social

relations, or take care of himself or herself. The disturbance of the thought processes may include bizarre delusions, hallucinations, incoherence, looseness of associations, or a flat or inappropriate emotional response. It is required that signs of the disturbance be present continuously for at least six months. A prodromal and a residual phase commonly precede and follow the active period. Five schizophrenic disorders are presently recognized:

(a) *Disorganized schizophrenic disorder*—further characterized by incoherence and inappropriate affect.

(b) *Catatonic schizophrenic disorder*—further characterized by rigidity, posturing, stupor, negativism, or uncontrollable excitement.

(c) *Paranoid schizophrenic disorder*—further characterized by systematized grandiose or persecutory delusions, delusions of jealousy, or auditory hallucinations with persecutory or grandiose content, without incoherence or disorganized thinking or behavior.

(d) *Undifferentiated schizophrenic disorder*—a term to be used when a schizophrenic individual cannot be characterized as belonging to any of the three types just described.

(e) *Residual schizophrenic disorder*—a term to be used with individuals who have reintegrated after presenting a clearly schizophrenic picture and who still show some residue of the previous symptomatology.

4. *Delusional (paranoid) disorder:* This disorder involves the presence of nonbizarre delusions of at least a month's duration without prominent hallucinations or bizarre behaviors. The following types are recognized:

(a) *Egomanic type*—the predominant delusion is that a person, usually of higher status, is in love with the subject.

(b) *Grandiose type*—the predominant theme is one of an inflated self-image.

(c) *Jealous type*—the belief is that one's sexual partner is unfaithful.

(d) *Persecutory type*—the complaint is of being mistreated or persecuted.

(e) *Somatic type*—the person is convinced that he or she has a physical disease.

(f) *Unspecified type.*

5. *Other psychoses*

(a) *Schizophreniform disorder*—a schizophrenia-like disorder of less than six months' duration in a person with no history of schizophrenia.

(b) *Schizoaffective disorder*—characterized by delusions or hallucinations of at least two weeks' duration, in the absence of prominent mood symptoms, in a person with a diagnosable affective disorder. Schizoaffective disorders can be bipolar or depressive type.

(c) *Induced (shared) psychotic disorder*—characterized by the appearance of a delusion as a response to a close relationship with a person who believes in that delusion.
(d) *Psychotic disorder not otherwise specified.*

6. *Mood disorders*
   (a) *Depressive episode*—characterized by a predominantly dysphoric mood or a loss of interest and pleasure for at least two weeks. It may also involve poor appetite and weight loss, a sleep disturbance, a loss of energy, guilt feelings, feelings of self-reproach, inability to concentrate, or recurrent morbid thoughts. Depressive episodes can be of the "melancholic" type if they are marked by a loss of interest, an inability to experience pleasure in life, anorexia and weight loss, psychomotor retardation or agitation, early morning awakening, or a depression that is worse in the morning.
   (b) *Depressive disorder, recurrent*—characterized by repeated episodes as just described.
   (c) *Dysthymic disorder*—depression of at least two years' duration that is not of sufficient severity to be classified as a depressive disorder. Dysthymia is usually associated with poor appetite or overeating, insomnia or hypersomnia, low energy, low self-esteem, poor concentration, inability to make decisions, or feelings of hopelessness. The diagnosis is applicable only when there have not been extended periods of time during which the disturbance was absent.
   (d) *Depression disorder not otherwise specified.*
   (e) *Bipolar disorder, manic phase*—characterized by a period of elevated, expansive, or irritable mood as exemplified by accelerated psychomotor activity, flight of ideas, inflated self-esteem, reduced sleep time, inability to concentrate, impulsive behavior, or excessive involvement in pleasurable activities.
   (f) *Bipolar disorder, depressive phase*—characterized as a depressive state in an individual who has also had manic episodes as just defined.
   (g) *Bipolar disorder, mixed*—characterized by the existence of both manic and depressive states that alternate every few days.
   (h) *Cyclothymic disorder*—consists of mild but chronic mood fluctuations. The cyclothymic disorder requires both depressed and elevated moods that are not substantial enough to qualify as a bipolar disorder but that have been present for at least two years. The diagnosis is applicable only when there have not been extended periods of time during which the disturbance was not present.
   (i) *Bipolar disorder not otherwise specified.*

The major mood disorders described may be accompanied by psychotic features. According to the DSM-III-R, such a clinical picture continues to represent a mood disorder unless there is a psychotic episode at a time when mood difficulties are not present (in which case the proper diagnosis would be schizoaffective disorder). The psychotic features are termed "mood congruent" or "mood incongruent" in accordance with whether they are consistent with the mood experienced by the individual (e.g., the delusion that one has a terrible disease and is about to die is "mood congruent" during a depressive episode; the delusion that one is an FBI agent would be "mood incongruent").

7. *Anxiety disorders*
   (a) *Panic disorder*—characterized by periods of extreme anxiety in response to a life threat or a phobic stimulus. The attacks may include shortness of breath, palpitations, chest pain, choking sensations, dizziness, feelings of unreality, skin sensations, sweating, nausea or abdominal distress, chills, tremors, or the fear of some impending danger. This disorder is found with or without agoraphobia (fear of places from which escape may be difficult).
   (b) *Generalized anxiety disorder*—characterized by the presence of an anxious mood which is in response to a significant environmental stress and which lasts six months or longer. The anxious mood may include tension, restlessness, tremors, fatigue, sweating, heart palpitations, stomach disturbances, shortness of breath, dry mouth, dizziness, chills, frequent urination, trouble swallowing, irritability, insomnia, inability to concentrate, or feelings of being keyed up or on edge.
   (c) *Obsessive-compulsive disorder*—characterized by the presence of obsessions (disturbing and recurrent thoughts that the individual cannot get out of his or her mind) or compulsions (behaviors that the individual feels have to be carried out if a catastrophic event is to be prevented) that interfere with the normal functioning of the individual.
   (d) *Simple phobia*—characterized by the presence of an irrational fear and avoidance of an object or situation to a degree that interferes with the individual's normal functioning. This category is used only when the disorder does not meet the criteria for agoraphobia or social phobia.
   (e) *Agoraphobia without panic disorder*—characterized by a fear of places from which escape may be difficult severe enough to restrict the person's life. Exposure to such a situation may be accompanied by dizziness, depersonalization, derealization, loss of bladder or bowel control, vomiting, or cardiac distress.

(f) *Social phobia*—characterized by a fear of social situations in which the person feels exposed to the scrutiny of others and fears acting in humiliating or embarrassing ways. The fear restricts the person's life, and exposure to such situations is accompanied by intense anxiety and discomfort.

(g) *Anxiety disorder not otherwise specified.*

8. *Factitious disorders:* A factitious disorder is characterized by the production of psychological or physical symptoms that are under the control of the individual and fulfill an emotional purpose in his or her life. Three such disorders are recognized:

(a) *Factitious disorder with physical symptoms*

(b) *Factitious disorder with psychological symptoms*

(c) *Factitious disorder not otherwise specified*

9. *Somatoform disorders:* These disorders are characterized by the presence, for at least six months, of somatic complaints that result from emotional factors (organic causes have been ruled out) and that do not appear to be under the conscious control of the individual. Somatoform disorders include the following types:

(a) *Somatoform pain disorder*—complaint exclusively involves pain.

(b) *Conversion disorder*—involves a loss or alteration of a physical function in an individual who does not have the somatization disorder.

(c) *Somatization disorder*—involves a lifelong pattern of serious medical complaints so that the individual has a dramatic, vague, and complicated medical history that has altered his or her lifestyle.

(d) *Hypochondriacal disorder*—characterized by unrealistic interpretations of normal sensations as indications of serious illness; these interpretations persist in spite of medical reassurance.

(e) *Body dysmorphic disorder*—involves the preoccupation with an exaggerated physical trait that is seen as a physical anomaly in a person of normal appearance.

(f) *Undifferentiated somatoform disorder*—involves one or more physical complaints in an individual who does not meet the criteria for another somatoform disorder.

(g) *Somatoform disorder not otherwise specified.*

10. *Dissociative disorders.*

(a) *Psychogenic amnesia*—characterized by the sudden inability to recall important personal information.

(b) *Psychogenic fugue*—characterized by a sudden move to a new place of residence, an inability to recall one's past, and an assumption of a new identity.

(c) *Multiple personality disorder*—characterized by the existence of more than one distinct personality, each having a complex set of behaviors, memories, and social associations, which recurrently take control of the person's behavior.

(d) *Depersonalization disorder*—characterized by an alteration in the individual's subjective experience of reality, so that the individual feels detached from himself or herself.

(e) *Dissociative disorder not otherwise specified.*

11. *Paraphilias:* This group of disorders is characterized by a disturbance of the sexual object so that the preferred method of sexual arousal involves an unusual sexual stimulus. In order for the problem to be diagnosable, the person has to be distressed by his or her choice of sexual object. This group includes the following disorders:

(a) *Pedophilia*—children are used to produce the sexual arousal.

(b) *Fetishism*—inanimate objects are used to produce the sexual arousal.

(c) *Exhibitionism*—the sexual arousal is accomplished through the exposure of the genitals to unsuspecting strangers.

(d) *Transvestic fetishism*—the sexual arousal in a heterosexual male without a gender identity disorder is accomplished through cross-dressing.

(e) *Voyeurism*—the sexual arousal is accomplished by looking at unsuspecting strangers when they are not fully dressed and with whom no further activity is sought.

(f) *Sexual masochism*—the sexual arousal is accomplished through intentional participation in an activity in which the individual is physically harmed.

(g) *Sexual sadism*—the sexual arousal is accomplished through intentional participation in an activity in which another individual is physically harmed.

(h) *Frotteurism*—when the sexual arousal is accomplished by touching or rubbing against a nonconsenting person.

(i) *Paraphilia not otherwise specified.*

12. *Sexual dysfunctions:* These disorders involve the persistent inability to obtain sexual fulfillment in cases in which this disturbance is not symptomatic of another emotional disorder.

(a) *Hypoactive sexual desire*—characterized by a lack of sexual desire.

(b) *Sexual aversion disorder*—characterized by aversion to and avoidance of sexual contact.

(c) *Female sexual arousal disorder*—characterized by a lack of sexual excitement after experiencing sexual desire or an inability to attain or maintain adequate lubrication.

(d) *Male erectile disorder*—involves a failure to attain or maintain an erection or a lack of sexual excitement after experiencing sexual desire.

(e) *Inhibited (female or male) orgasm*—characterized by an inability to reach a sexual orgasm after an adequate sexual encounter and after experiencing both sexual desire and excitement.

(f) *Premature ejaculation*—an absence of reasonable voluntary control of the sexual orgasm in males.

(g) *Dyspareunia*—characterized by the presence of pain during sexual intercourse.

(h) *Vaginismus*—involuntary spasms in the vagina that interfere with sexual activity.

(i) *Sexual dysfunction not otherwise specified.*

13. *Dyssomnias:* Dyssomnias are diagnosed when there is a disturbance of the sleep pattern that has been present several times a week for a month or more. This disturbance must be accompanied by problems during the day that are attributable to the sleep disturbance, such as fatigue or irritability. These disorders include:

(a) *Insomnia* (insufficient sleep time) *related to another mental disorder.*

(b) *Insomnia related to a known organic factor.*

(c) *Primary insomnia* (when it is neither of the above).

(d) *Hypersomnia* (excessive sleep time) *related to another mental disorder.*

(e) *Hypersomnia related to a known organic factor.*

(f) *Primary hypersomnia.*

(g) *Sleep-wake schedule disorder* (change of the sleep-wake pattern not involving excessive or insufficient sleep); this disorder has three different types: advance-delayed, disorganized, and frequent changing.

(h) *Dyssomnia not otherwise specified*

14. *Parasomnias:* Parasomnias are diagnosed when there is a disturbance that repeatedly occurs during sleep that is not related to the sleep pattern itself but that causes the person distress. They include:

(a) *Dream anxiety disorder*—characterized by awakenings during frightening dreams, without confusion or disorientation upon awakening.

(b) *Sleep fervor disorder*—characterized by abrupt awakenings accompanied by a scream and intense anxiety, unresponsiveness, and disorientation lasting several minutes.

(c) *Sleepwalking disorder*—characterized by arising from bed and walking with a blank facial expression. Upon awakening, the person is amnesic of the episode but shows good recovery of other intellectual functions after a brief period of time.

(d) *Parasomnia not otherwise specified.*

15. *Impulse control disorders:* These disorders are characterized by the inability to resist harmful impulses in cases in which this disturbance is not symptomatic of another emotional disorder. This group includes:

(a) *Pathological gambling*—characterized by a preoccupation and urge to gamble and a pleasure in gambling irresponsibly with large amounts of money.

(b) *Kleptomania*—involves the impulse to steal when the pleasure is obtained from the act of stealing rather than from any material gain.

(c) *Pyromania*—involves the urge to set fires when the pleasure obtained does not come from any practical gain for the individual.

(d) *Intermittent explosive disorder*—diagnosed when violent aggressive attacks have resulted in serious assaultive acts or destruction of property.

(e) *Trichotillomania*—characterized by an impulse to pull one's own hair, resulting in noticeable hair loss; the impulse is preceded by an increase of tension and followed by a sense of relief.

(f) *Impulse control disorder not otherwise specified.*

II.E. REACTIVE DISORDERS

The reactive disorders consist of symptoms resulting from an environmental situation that is abnormally difficult. The symptoms may include both exaggerations of the basic personality style and ego-dystonic complaints. They are treated in this *Manual* separately from the clinical syndromes, since they are thought to be mainly a result of environmental stresses. The DSM-III-R, however, makes little distinction between these disorders and the clinical syndromes, places them on the same axis (Axis I), and does not even group all the reactive disorders together.

For the purpose of the present work, the reactive disorders will be classified in three groups:

(a) Nonpsychotic symptoms resulting from a traumatic situation or catastrophic occurrence, called post-traumatic stress disorders.

(b) Nonpsychotic symptoms resulting from noncatastrophic environmental stress, classified as adjustment disorders.

(c) Psychotic symptoms resulting from environmental stresses, referred to as brief psychotic reactions.

The reactive disorder diagnoses are not used when the presenting symptoms are an exacerbation of an emotional disorder that was present prior to the onset of the stress.

1. *Post-traumatic stress disorder:* The post-traumatic stress disorder develops after the occurrence of a traumatic event and is characterized by recurrent recollections or dreams about the event, persistent avoidance of stimuli associated with this trauma, and persistent symptoms of increased arousal, such as a sleep disturbance or irritability.

2. *Adjustment disorders:* These disorders are characterized by symptomatology severe enough to impair the individual's social or occupational
   functioning that is judged to be a reaction to an identifiable stressing
   situation, with onset occurring within three months of exposure to the
   stressor. The adjustment disorders are classified as follows:
   (a) *Adjustment disorder with depressed mood*
   (b) *Adjustment disorder with anxious mood*
   (c) *Adjustment disorder with mixed emotional features*
   (d) *Adjustment disorder with physical complaints*
   (e) *Adjustment disorder with disturbance of conduct*
   (f) *Adjustment disorder with mixed disturbance of emotion and conduct*
   (g) *Adjustment disorder with withdrawal*
   (h) *Adjustment disorder with work inhibition*
   (i) *Adjustment disorder not otherwise specified*

3. *Brief reactive psychosis:* This disorder is characterized by a brief period
   of incoherence, loosening of associations, delusions, hallucinations, or
   disorganization of behavior and emotional turmoil appearing shortly
   after a stressing environmental situation.

II.F CLINICAL SYNDROMES IN CHILDREN AND ADOLESCENTS

The syndromes presented in this section are mixed in etiology, the only
commonality being their origination in childhood or adolescence. They
include deficits due to organicity, such as the mental retardations; impairments due to exaggerations or personality patterns, such as the conduct disorders; and symptoms that are added on to the basic personality structure,
such as eating disorders.

The issue in grouping these syndromes together is further complicated by
the fact that they are not seen exclusively in children. For instance, although
the eating disorders are typically seen in adolescence, an adult onset of such
a disorder is occasionally encountered. Moreover, children and adolescents
often suffer from disorders that are not included in this group (e.g., depressions).
In either one of these cases, when the person meets the criteria for a
particular disorder, that diagnosis should be used. The only exceptions to
this rule are the personality disorders, which are not typically diagnosed
in childhood or adolescence since they require that the pattern of behavior
continue into adulthood.

Table 5 shows the basic classification scheme. All of these disorders are
coded on Axis I, except for the specific developmental disorders, which are
coded on Axis II.

TABLE 5. Disorders of Childhood and Adolescence

No.	Disease Group	Basic Characteristic
1	Mental retardation	Low overall intellectual ability
2	Pervasive developmental diseases	Severe overall lack of development
3	Specific developmental disorders	Lack of development in specific area
4	Attention deficit disorders	Difficulty maintaining attention
5	Disruptive disorders	Disciplinary problems
6	Anxiety disorders	Anxiety and tension
7	Eating disorders	Disturbance in eating behaviors
8	Gender identity disorders	Discomfort with one's gender
9	Tic disorders	Repetitive movements or vocalizations
10	Elimination disorders	Disturbance in urine or fecal control
11	Other disorders	

1. *Mental retardations:* These disorders are characterized by a significantly subaverage general intellectual ability. They are classified according to levels as follows:
   (a) *Mild mental retardation* — IQ from 55 to 69.
   (b) *Moderate mental retardation* — IQ from 35 to 54.
   (c) *Severe mental retardation* — IQ from 20 to 34.
   (d) *Profound mental retardation* — IQ less than 20.
   (e) *Unspecified mental retardation* — IQ not available.

2. *Pervasive developmental disorders* (to be coded on Axis II): These disorders are characterized by a severe lack of overall development in a child. They include:
   (a) *Autistic disorder* — characterized by lack of responsiveness to other humans, gross deficits in language development, and markedly restricted repertoire of activities and interests.
   (b) *Pervasive developmental disorder not otherwise specified.*

3. *Specific developmental disorders:* These disorders are characterized by a lack of development in one specific area of growth that is not due to inadequate learning opportunities or another physical or mental disorder (mental retardation must be ruled out). The particular types are as follows:
   (a) *Developmental reading disorder* — characterized by a reading learning disability.
   (b) *Developmental arithmetical disorder* — characterized by an arithmetical learning disability.
   (c) *Developmental receptive language disorder* — characterized by a learning disability of language comprehension.

(d) *Developmental expressive language disorder*—characterized by an expressive language disability in an individual who has acceptable receptive language.

(e) *Developmental expressive writing disorder*—characterized by a lack of development of writing skills.

(f) *Developmental articulation disorder*—characterized by a misarticulation of speech sounds.

(g) *Developmental coordination disorder*—characterized by motor coordination markedly behind that expected for the person's age.

(h) *Specific developmental disorder not otherwise specified.*

4. *Attention deficit disorders:* These disorders involve difficulty maintaining attention, following instructions, staying on task, or playing quietly. The disturbance must have lasted for at least six months. These disorders can be of two types:

(a) *Attention-deficit hyperactivity disorder*—accompanied by hyperactivity, impulsivity, and low frustration tolerance.

(b) *Undifferentiated attention-deficit disorder*—an attention deficit disorder without hyperactivity.

5. *Disruptive behavior disorders*

(a) *Conduct disorder*—characterized by criminal behavior, disciplinary difficulties, and physical aggressiveness. Three types are recognized: group, solitary-aggressive, and undifferentiated.

(b) *Oppositional-defiant disorder*—characterized by pervasive and persistent oppositional, negativistic, and provocative behaviors when the behavior is not symptomatic of a conduct disorder, a psychotic disorder, or a mood disorder.

6. *Anxiety disorders:* These are disorders in which the predominant symptom is the presence of anxiety. Three types are presently recognized:

(a) *Separation anxiety disorder*—characterized by persistent fears that something bad would happen if the child were separated from his family, and the presence of emotional distress when the child is separated.

(b) *Avoidant disorder of childhood or adolescence*—characterized by persistent shyness, for a period of at least six months, in a child who is at least 2½ years old. The shyness has to be severe enough to interfere with the ability to function with peers in an individual who has warm and satisfying relationships in the family.

(c) *Overanxious disorder*—characterized by persistent worrying about past or future events and concern about self-competence, accompanied by somatic complaints or excessive need for reassurance.

7. *Eating disorders:* Eating disorders are characterized by a disturbance in the child's eating behavior. The different types follow:
   (a) *Anorexia nervosa*—characterized by a fear of becoming obese, together with a disturbance of body image and significant weight loss. The weight loss is due to either refusal to eat appropriate amounts of food or self-induced vomiting.
   (b) *Bulimia nervosa*—characterized by binges during which large amounts of food are consumed in a short period of time, as well as attempts to prevent weight gain through self-induced vomiting, use of laxatives, or the like.
   (c) *Pica*—characterized by the ingestion of nonedible substances.
   (d) *Rumination*—characterized by self-induced vomiting with resulting weight loss in an individual who does not have anorexia nervosa.
   (e) *Eating disorder not otherwise specified.*

8. *Gender identity disorders*
   (a) *Gender identity disorder of childhood*—characterized by persistent and intense distress with one's own sex, a preference for clothes that simulate those typical of the opposite sex, and repudiation of sexual anatomical structures (e.g., assertions that one will eventually grow opposite-sex genitals, that one's sexual organs are disgusting, or the like).
   (b) *Transsexualism*—characterized by a persistent discomfort with one's own sex and a preoccupation with acquiring the sexual characteristics of the opposite sex in a person who has already reached puberty.
   (c) *Gender identity disorder of adolescence or adulthood, nontranssexual type*—characterized by a persistent discomfort with one's own sex and recurrent cross-dressing, not done for the purpose of sexual excitement, by a person who has already reached puberty.
   (d) *Gender identity disorder not otherwise specified.*

9. *Tic disorders:* The disorders that follow involve repetitive, stereotyped, and involuntary movements or volcalizations that can be voluntarily suppressed only for a period of time and that usually diminish during sleep. They include:
   (a) *Tic disorder* (can be transient or chronic).
   (b) *Tourette's disorder*—consists of both motor *and* vocal tics.
   (c) *Tic disorder not otherwise specified.*

10. *Elimination disorder:* The disorders that follow involve difficulties with the control of elimination in children who are at least 4 years of age. The episodes must happen at least once a month for a period of six months and cannot be due to a physical disorder.

(a) *Functional encopresis*—characterized by the voiding of feces.

(b) *Functional enuresis*—characterized by the voiding of urine.

11. *Other disorders of childhood and adolescence*

(a) *Reactive attachment disorder of infancy*—develops after a gross lack of care for the infant and is characterized by a lack of development of social responsiveness (e.g., lack of visual tracking of faces, no smiling). The disorder is accompanied by a withdrawn existence (e.g., weak cry, excessive sleep) and weight loss. The diagnosis is used only in cases in which the disturbance is not due to another disorder.

(b) *Elective mutism*—characterized by a continuous and persistent refusal to speak to most other persons when the refusal is not symptomatic of another disorder.

(c) *Identity disorder*—disorder of late adolescence characterized by a subjective distress over uncertainty about self-identity or goals.

(d) *Stuttering.*

(e) *Cluttering*—rapid, erratic, and dysrhythmic speech that groups words in ways that are not consistent with the grammatical structure of the sentence.

(f) *Stereotyping habit disorder*—characterized by intentional, repetitive, nonfunctional behaviors (such as nail biting, hand washing) that cause physical injury or interfere with normal activities.

III The Diagnostic Interview

III.A. INTRODUCTION

Most psychologists feel that it is necessary to become knowledgeable about the client before any recommendations can be made. This is so because clients come with a variety of problems, goals for treatment, strengths, and degrees of ability to change. Moreover, clinical settings have become differentiated in what they can offer, so that an effort has to be made to provide a good fit between the client and the service provider. Finally, clinicians are frequently asked to see a client with the exclusive purpose of providing a psychological evaluation. The diagnostic interview is the procedure most often used in order to assess a client.

The primary purpose of the diagnostic interview is to gather information about the client. The interview may also serve to establish a relationship, provide reassurance, and so on. However, the primary goal of gathering information will be emphasized in this *Manual* almost to the exclusion of all other goals.

Two important aspects of the diagnostic interview are:
  (a) The content—the actual information that is needed from the patient as well as the examiner's evaluation of the patient's psychological functioning (mental status).
  (b) The method or process through which the information is obtained.

The body of the interview should be preceded by preliminary remarks that serve to:
  (a) Establish rapport and set the patient at ease.
  (b) Clarify the purpose of the interview.
  (c) Answer any questions that the patient may have about the procedure.

The information to be obtained from the patient should include:
  (a) The presenting complaint—what problems the patient is having, how long he or she has had these problems, and why help is being sought at this time. Attention should be directed toward getting an accurate and specific description of the complaints. The statement that the person is "depressed" or has "bad nerves," for example, should be pursued further, since those terms mean very different things to different people. Thus, the interviewer should learn what specific

39

symptoms (e.g., feeling sad, crying easily, a loss of appetite) the client is experiencing.

(b) The present life situation—where does the patient live and with whom; how are the relationships of the different members of the household.

(c) The mental health history—what emotional problems the patient has had in the past; what treatment, if any, was received and how effective it was; how much the person drinks and if there is any history of other substance abuse; whether the person has any relatives who have suffered from significant emotional problems.

(d) The medical history—any major medical illness or any accidents that the individual has had and any present disabilities from which the patient suffers.

(e) The family history—a brief account of the family of origin and the major events of the person's childhood. The history of any marriages and any children that he or she has had.

(f) Social history—the relationships that the patient has had or presently has outside of his family; significant sexual experiences of the past.

(g) Educational and occupational history—the extent of education and training together with the kind of jobs that the person has held.

The clinical observations made during the diagnostic interview and the information obtained are often sufficient to evaluate many aspects of the patient's functioning. A good interviewer pays much attention to the nonverbal behavior of the client and what these behaviors may be communicating. Eye contact, physical distance, gestures, facial expressions, and body movements have been emphasized in the literature. Further procedures to be followed in order to complete a "mental status examination" will be discussed in the next section.

The usual strategy in a diagnostic interview is to prompt the patient to talk about one of the areas just described with a general, open-ended question (e.g., "How can I help you?" "Could you tell me about your family?" and so on). The advantages of the general, open-ended question are that:

(a) It does not take time away from the patient with lengthy questions by the interviewer. Johnson (1981, p. 83) stated that "it is usually the overanxious, inexperienced interviewer who spends a significant portion of the interview speaking rather than listening."

(b) It gives some control of the interview to the patient, so that the patient has more of a chance to demonstrate how he or she functions. The patient will then organize the answers in his or her unique way, giving clues about personality style, level of pathology, and so on.

(c) It allows the patient to choose the areas that she or he is most concerned with.

If the patient stops talking before an area is covered, further promptings may be appropriate. These may take the form of:

(a) Silence, giving the patient time to think and continue the narrative.
(b) An encouraging gesture like a nod, a "yes," or something similar.
(c) A verbal request for more information, like "Go on, please" or "Could you tell me more about that?"
(d) A reflective statement that echoes what the patient has said, usually underlying the feelings involved, like "You felt hurt when your girlfriend forgot your birthday."
(e) A summary statement, like "Up to now you have told me the difficulties that you are having at work. Can you tell me more about your life?"
(f) An interpretation, like "You seem to want to avoid talking about this. Do you have any feelings about sharing it with me?"
(g) A statement of support or reassurance, in the case of a fearful or uneasy patient.
(h) A confrontation, like "The judge told you that you had to see me, but you really don't want to talk to me."
(i) A self-disclosure may be used when a patient seems really afraid of revealing himself or herself in a sensitive area. Such self-disclosure may help him or her feel less vulnerable.

The goal of any of these promptings is only to encourage further disclosure. As a result, the less intrusive or extensive a prompting is, the more effective it may be. The first few types of interventions given above (silences, encouraging gestures, etc.) are much preferred. Statements of support, confrontations, and self-disclosures should be used infrequently and only after other attempts have failed.

There are times, however, when the interviewer should switch from the open-ended questions to more specific ones. This switch is particularly appropriate when:

(a) The patient appears lost with the more general prompting and needs more guidance.
(b) It has already been established that the patient handles the general, open-ended questions by giving tangential or irrelevant answers that do not add further information.
(c) The patient has already covered an area but has left out some details that the interviewer sees as important.

In these cases, the specific questions should be asked in a direct and clear manner but without suggesting answers to the patient.

In instances when a confused or noninsightful patient is being interviewed, even direct, specific questions may not bring out the information wanted. In some occasions, the use of multiple choice questioning is appropriate. Some individuals are then able to pick the choice they feel answers the questions best.

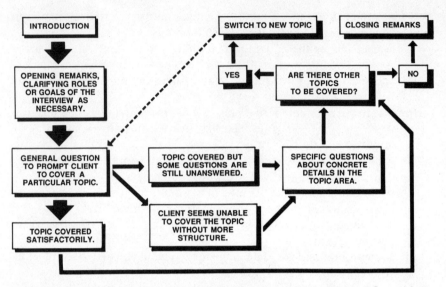

Figure 3. Flow Chart for Diagnostic Interviews. (Adapted from Richard Greenblatt, unpublished work.)

After an area has been covered, the interviewer should switch to a new area, usually using again the more general and open-ended questioning technique. Figure 3 maps out the proposed plan for a diagnostic interview.

The following events are to be avoided, since they usually do not lead to a productive information-gathering process:

(a) Questions that antagonize the patient.
(b) Questions that provide an answer. It is better to ask, "How were you feeling?" than, "Were you feeling nervous?"
(c) "Machine gunning" (asking one question after another without giving time to respond).
(d) Prolonged silences.
(e) A situation in which the patient is allowed to go on talking while the interviewer is not paying attention.
(f) Any situation that makes the patient feel ill at ease, shamed, embarrassed, rejected, humiliated, or the like.

The reader is referred to Section V.E. for a review of difficult situations in handling patients. There are, however, some difficult situations that are specific to the interview. These include: (a) the verbose or overtalkative client, (b) the nontalker, (c) the confused or incoherent patient, and (d) the tangential or circumstantial patient.

With the overtalkative patient the following suggestions may be useful:
(a) Share the task that has to be accomplished (getting the needed

information) and the time available; in this way one enlists the patient's help so that it becomes a collaborative enterprise in which the patient is also involved.

(b) As you learn more about the patient, an interpretation can be attempted: Does he talk more when he is anxious? Does she talk more when discussing a particular area of her life situation? This approach can be followed with interpretations when the patient starts talking excessively again.

(c) Reinforce the patient by demonstrating your appreciation when he or she gives a concise answer.

With the nontalker, the trick is usually to figure out why the patient does not talk. Likely options are:

(a) Extreme fear or confusion.

(b) Paranoid suspiciousness.

(c) Anger—this is particularly likely when the patient is forced to meet with the interviewer.

(d) An organic impairment.

The cause of the lack of communication may be determined by:

(a) Spending some time with the patient.

(b) Asking the patient why he or she doesn't want to talk. Some reasons can be tentatively suggested if the patient does not respond.

The confused patient can be helped by asking questions that call for short and concrete answers.

The tangential or circumstantial patient may be handled using the same suggestions presented for the overtalkative patient.

Most interviews end with some closing remarks. These remarks serve to:

(a) Answer any questions that the client may have.

(b) Clarify how the information will be handled or what the next step in obtaining help may be.

(c) When necessary, help the client regain his or her composure.

An attitude of warmth and understanding should prevail throughout the interview. The clinician should attempt to come through in a professional manner but as an individual who is interested in the patient and will behave in an honest and predictable way. A problem that some inexperienced interviewers have is that they try to "be a friend" to the client or help the patient along the way. A stance that denotes a professional distance and objectivity is actually more helpful in allowing the patient to reveal himself or herself than an attempt on the part of the interviewer to become more intimate. For more comments regarding what constitutes a recommended interpersonal approach for a psychologist, see Section V.D.

Recommended references on the subject of diagnostic interviewing are the books by Bernstein, Bernstein, and Dana (1974), Froelich and Bishop (1977), MacKinnon and Michels (1971), and Molyneaux and Lane (1982).

III.B.   THE MENTAL STATUS EXAMINATION

The mental status examination involves an assessment of how well the patient is able to process information and function. It is important to carry out such an assessment as part of the diagnostic interview because significant deficiencies in the client's functioning have to be taken into consideration for the recommendations to be appropriate. Moreover, neurological disorders may first surface as complaints that sound like emotional disorders.

At first sight, the examination suggested below may appear involved and time-consuming. In fact, an adequate mental status exam does not take much more than five additional minutes in the case of a patient who is intellectually intact. This is so because many of the areas mentioned can be evaluated without additional time expenditure by observing how the patient handles the questions during the course of the interview. The mental status examination is further helped by the fact that most tasks have a hierarchical distribution. In other words, if a person cannot subtract fifty cents from one dollar, he or she is not going to be able to perform a complicated division. The most effective strategy with a client who seems intellectually intact is to present first the more difficult tasks for each of the areas given below; if the person is able to do the more difficult screening task, the easier items can be skipped.

The areas of assessment are:

1. Appearance: Physical characteristics, the formality and appropriateness of the patient's clothes, cleanliness, etc.

2. Alertness: Is the patient unduly sleepy or lethargic?

3. Orientation: Does the patient know where he is, the time and date, who you are and who he is?

4. Coherence: Can the patient speak in sentences that make sense?

5. Attention and concentration: Can the patient keep track of the questions asked? Can she repeat four digits without difficulty?

6. Sensation and perception: Can the patient see and hear well?

7. Language: Can the patient understand what is said without problem? Can he name objects without delay (e.g., the different parts of a watch: face, wristband, buckle, crystal, stem)? Can she repeat words and short sentences? Can she read and spell adequately?

8. Memory: Can the patient remember recent and past events? Give the patient three words (e.g., Cadillac, zebra, and purple) and see if she can remember them five minutes later. Ask her to name the last four presidents of the United States, starting with the present.

9. Planning and mental control: Can the patient plan his answers effectively? Can he recite backward the months of the year or do serial counting (counting by 3's or by 7's)?

10. Abstractions: Simple tasks include giving two different meanings for a word (e.g., right, left, bit). Idioms are more difficult (e.g., What would I mean if I said I was feeling blue? What would I mean if I said I was seeing red? How about if I said someone had a chip on his shoulder? Or if I said someone was hot under the collar?). Still more difficult are proverbs (e.g., Rome wasn't built in a day; A stitch in time saves nine; A rolling stone gathers no moss; In the land of the blind, the one-eyed is king).

11. Calculations: Simple tasks include subtracting $1.62 from $5.00 or $2.77 out of $10.00; more complicated are multiplications, like 43×57.

12. Figure reproductions: Simple tasks may be a square, a triangle, or the Greek cross; more complicated is drawing a three-dimensional cube.

13. Thought process: Should include the manner of approach (global or detail); the organization; the logic; the degree of clarity and differentiation; and the control demonstrated in the thinking process. Is there evidence of loose associations or poor judgment?

14. Thought content: Should include the apparent level of reality testing, the relevance of the thinking, the appropriateness of the thoughts, and the amount of insight demonstrated.

15. Affective response: Is the emotional response consistent with the content of the conversation?

16. Mood: Describe the prevailing mood as happy, sad, despondent, melancholic, etc. Make a statement about the hopefulness or pessimism that the patient demonstrates, when relevant.

17. Anxiety level: Note the level of tension or nervousness and the way in which the patient handles the anxiety, his or her defense mechanisms, etc.

18. Motor activity: Speech rate, ability to sit still, and level of energy that the patient has available.

19. Predominant defense mechanism if such was noticed during the interview.

20. Relationship toward the examiner: Was the patient open, friendly, and cooperative? Did any problems like mistrust, hostility, excessive shyness, or the like appear during the session?

The book by Strub and Black (1977) is highly recommended.

III.C. A DIAGNOSTIC INTERVIEW

A transcript of an interview follows. An interview like the one below with a cooperative patient should not take more than 30 minutes even when it is done at an unhurried and easy pace. Practically all of the areas of inquiry could have been explored further, but the brevity of this interview serves to demonstrate how expediently the needed information can be obtained. The author's comments in reviewing the interview later on are shown in italics.

I: Hello. I am _____. How can I help you?
P: Well, I don't know. A lot of strange things are going on and stuff without the . . . I was with this, I was the last few months . . . I've been hearing people tell me I must be crazy, I must be a nut. So after two weeks went by, I decided to come into the hospital. It seemed strange to me that at one time everything I was doing struck me as though somebody was making notes or notations of it and then, in an indirect way, like a third person, they would be talking to one another and I would be the third person but I would hear what was being said and I could relate to what they were talking about but yet, they would vary the conversation to the extent that they would talk about different people or different places. When they came right down to the subject of whatever it is that they were talking about, it would be a completely different subject altogether but yet it was something that I could associate with or relate to.

The interview starts with a brief question, expressed in a serious and profes-sional tone. The opening question is very general. The tone throughout the interview attempts to be one of warmth and understanding. In this brief segment the patient has already shown ideas of reference, feelings of depersonalization, confusion about himself, and an inability to express himself with clarity.

I: Had this ever happened to you before?
P: No.

Interviewer questions about past emotional disturbances.

I: How old are you?
P: Twenty-four.
I: So about two months ago you started feeling that strange things were happening.

The interviewer felt that he needed to know the client's age in order to place the information in perspective. Then he gets the patient back into talking about the presenting complaint with a general prompting.

P: Well, that took . . . three or four months ago. Yes. I don't know what really is behind it all, other than the fact that I was told that if I can't find out through the people who I'm with, I might as well go to the hospital and let them tell me what's wrong and they could probably, they would be able to straighten out the situation and tell me what's going on.

I: What about prior to this time? Have you ever thought of yourself as needing help for some emotional problem?

P: No.

I: Have you ever seen a psychiatrist or a psychologist before?

The interviewer inquires again about past mental health problems. Given the degree of pathology, he found it hard to believe that the client had never received treatment before.

P: No, I haven't. . . . Not a psychiatrist. . . . I mean I may have talked to an analyst and not really been aware of it and yet . . . when I did come to Chicago myself, I had a rather difficult time trying to establish whom I was talking to. I came here looking for one of two things: a police officer or a priest, and nobody wanted to identify with one or another, nobody wanted to be one or the other.

Patient continues to show confusion and tangentiality in his train of thought.

I: When was it that you came to Chicago?

P: Roughly three months ago.

I: Where are you staying?

P: At the "Y."

I: Do you know anyone in this area?

P: No.

I: What were you doing before?

Interviewer moves into recent past.

P: I was in Michigan, in the U.P., which is the Upper Peninsula. I messed around and expired or used up all of my, what do you call it? . . . unemployment. So I ended up looking for three jobs, work at [name of store], working at a factory area and I can't recall working at where else, while I was there in Michigan. I do remember the time when I traveled downstate for two hours, where my folks are, where I completed high school, and I went through the employment officer and got a job through them working as a painter. I was painting there. They were working under contract and I was working as a painter myself. I painted the roof and the pipes that were up there. I don't know, something like 45 feet, 50 feet, up above, 50 feet off the ground.

I: Where were you born and raised?
P: In Kansas.
I: And when did you leave home?
P: When I went into the service.
I: How old were you then?
P: About nineteen.
I: How long did you go to school?
P: I finished high school.
I: What kind of student were you?
P: Good.
I: Were you ever in a special education class or having difficulties passing your subjects?
P: No.
I: How long did you spend in the service?
P: Three years, 11 months, and 20-some-odd days.
I: (Laughing) You got 'em all counted up! How was it?
P: I really didn't enjoy it. I didn't enjoy seeing all the things I saw going on and I was anxiously waiting to get out. I knew I had a four-year commitment and I didn't think I would attain the benefits that I would receive if I went about and took an early out. They tried twice and on their second attempt they managed to put me out by at least eight days early. Something happened to their paperwork and they didn't succeed the first time so they put it through again the second time.

The interviewer continues to move into the patient's history. First he uses some specific questions to place the information in perspective, but he soon asks a general question regarding the service and allows the patient to go on. The patient continued to show problems communicating clearly (e.g., he meant to say that the time had expired instead of saying that he had expired, and demonstrated uncertain and unsystematized paranoid thinking).

I: Did they kick you out?
P: No, I received an honorable discharge.
I: After finishing your time?
P: Yes.
I: So, what's this about managing to get you out before your time?

The interviewer asks some specific questions in order to clarify what actually happened.

P: That's rather strange. I would say some of the individuals in there didn't really care for me, some of the people who were in the position of authority. I know that at one time, one of my supervisors whom I got along with, had a favorable attitude towards me. His supervisor didn't particularly care for me, who was a civilian. When I got out of the service, I was an equipment operator, that was the last job I performed while I was in the service. He was a civilian and he didn't really object to me and in fact he, I had the impression that he was really trying to help me as best he could. But he worked under a civilian who really didn't care one way or the other. He was out to do his job. His senior, this superior, was a major and I had the impression that he didn't particularly care for the major, in his branch. His superior was a lieutenant colonel; again, he was doing his job.

The patient responds in a tangential manner and shows great uncertainty. The paranoid ideation is, nevertheless, indisputable.

I: So what did they gain by putting you out?
P: Well, stopping my ideals, my attitudes, my thoughts. Because, see what they did is, they took me from my job, my working situation, and because they couldn't put anything on me, or nail me with anything, they, and they didn't have any solid reason for just putting me out of the service, they put me in a situation and an environment where I had very little exposure to people. They put me in an equipment crib, I recognized this to be a made-up job. I had to record in a simple notebook paper who was taking out shovels and equipment. The paper was not regulation form, was simple stationery.
I: And this was the job that they put you to do because they didn't like you, wanted to stop your ideals and wanted to get rid of you.
P: Yes, this is the job they gave me to do until my time ran out.
I: So, after you finished, then what happened?
P: I moved downtown. I went to the nearest city in Michigan and put in an application to do some type of work. Then, when I realized that I wasn't going to get any job, I realized that the next best thing for me to do was to leave the area and look for work elsewhere.

The interviewer questions the patient in order to fill the gap between the service time and the recent past.

I: Where did you go?

P: Here.

(Brief silence)

I: But, in the meantime, you were able to work for [name of store]?

P: I worked one day! My part-time jobs never consisted of two or three days. The longest job I held was when I decided to go home, down in Kansas, and I worked from the 27th of December until the 3rd of January. I was making $6.20 an hour. I imagine that that was because of the holidays. I said $2.20 an hour, isn't that what I said? Wait a minute, $2.50 an hour? . . . I don't even remember what it was!

(Brief silence)

The patient clarifies the job issue. The impression now is that he has been functioning very poorly and has been unable to hold on to the jobs that he has been able to acquire.

I: Tell me a little bit about your family.

P: About my family?

I: Uh hum.

The interviewer shifts the topic in order to get at the family background.

P: Well, I rather not talk about my family, you know, because . . . all I would say is that our family, we don't see eye to eye, we don't get along. . . .

The patient objects at first but then goes on.

I: Who's at home?

P: My parents, and I have two sisters, they are younger than I am.

(Brief silence)

I: And you had trouble getting along with all of them?

P: Well, my own opinion is that my father was harder on me because I was older and he gave in to my youngest sister because he treated her as the baby of the family.

(Brief silence)

I: Do you know of any members of your family who have been hospitalized for psychiatric problems?

P: No.

I: Are there any members of your family who have a drinking problem or who abuse drugs?

P: No.

The interviewer returns with specific questions in order to get more informa-
tion about the family.

I: So, when you went into the service, things were not going well at home.
P: No. I went into the service to get away and make a life on my own. It
   seems like things didn't go well at all. I went in to make a twenty-year
   career out of it but things didn't go well at all.
I: How come?
P: How come? I imagine that it has to do with the people I became involved
   with and associated with while I was in service. I imagine, I am not really
   sure. It seems like someone was always having a turn or a play about what
   was going on with my life.

The interviewer sees a chance to tap, once more, into the events that took
place in the Army. This turns out to be wasted time, since the patient returns
to the paranoid ideas.

I: Have you ever been in the hospital before?
P: I was treated a few times, yes.
I: What was the problem?
P: Well, the most distinctive time I recall was ah, a brain scan, something
   that took place after I cross-trained. See, when I first enlisted I went into
   a career field known as a "weapons mechanic" which is nothing more
   than a "bomb jockey" better known as a "bomb loader." I loaded weapons in aircraft, and I got into problems with the law in relations to
   marijuana, and through that, it took place four or five months after I got
   to [military base] and that situation brought about a change in my career
   status. They pointed out that I had the option of getting out of the service
   or cross-training. I selected three different jobs that I wanted to go into,
   now that I couldn't be a weapons mechanic because what they found in
   my car was 12.5 grams of marijuana which is nearly estimated as enough
   to roll two joints. This was the evidence of the crime of what I considered
   my friend, he placed it in my car instead of sticking it in his pocket and
   when they searched the car, that's what they found. And, in spite of the
   fact that it was his, because it was in my car, I received credit for it. I was
   held for being in possession of it.
I: Were you given medications while you were in the hospital?
P: Yes.
I: Do you know the name of the medication you took?
P: No.
I: Did you continue to take it after you were discharged from the hospital?
P: No.

I: Do you know what the results were?
P: No.
I: Have you ever been told that you had a major medical illness of any kind?
P: No.
I: Do you see yourself as being physically healthy at this time?
P: Yes.

The patient admits to having previous medical or psychiatric problems and to being in the hospital, but he is clearly very defensive about it and cannot clarify what was happening with him. It would seem, however, that it may have been a psychiatric problem that had precipitated the previous admissions. An incident involving a drug charge is then narrated in an equally defensive manner.

I: Do you take drugs?
P: No. I used to smoke pot a long time ago.
I: Only pot?
P: Yes.
I: And when was the last time you smoked it?
P: Two . . . no. About four or five months ago.
   (Brief silence)

The interviewer asks specific questions to rule out the possibility of drug abuse. The patient denies significant drug abuse, but it is obvious by now that he may be unreliable.

I: I noticed that you are carrying a Bible. Are you a pretty religious fellow?
P: No. I am not a very religious fella. I turn to the Bible because it reveals many things to me. I found that the situation I'm in is not totally of my own doing. I realize that I was goaded into a situation where it doesn't matter which way I go. It reminds me a little bit of the service. All the alternatives have been considered and all the objectives for any alternative have been ruled out. Now, as a weak Bible believer or a weak person . . . and the faith of God . . . what will occur is once again this. . . . It isn't the first time that I pick up the Bible and read it following out what may be considered a weak Bible believer. What will occur next is for me to start backsliding, more or less meaning that I will regress back into the same old rut or the same plot or position I was at.

The interviewer moves into yet another area by sharing an observation and then asking a general question. The patient's response shows probable ideas of reference, a paranoid attitude, the thinking that he is always being placed

*in a situation that has no choices, confused thinking, and religiosity with
illogical reasons for it. Finally, there is the interesting association of religiosity with "backsliding," perhaps a bit of an insight; however, the patient was so
defensive the rest of the time that he surely would deny that he had been
"backsliding" at this time if asked.*

(At this point the interviewer spent a few minutes checking briefly a few
areas of the intellectual functioning that had not been tapped during the
interview. Thus, the patient was given three words to remember and was
asked to give the names of the last four presidents of the United States; he
was asked to do a few math problems; he was asked to read some sentences,
repeat some sentences, and reproduce some geometric figures. When he
failed to explain two proverbs he was asked to explain several idioms, a task
that he was able to do well. The patient also failed to give the different parts
of the watch, claiming that he had never "studied" watches, but named
successfully and without delay different parts of the interviewer's clothes
and objects around the examining room.)

I: OK. Unfortunately, we have to stop at this time. What I would like to do is
    arrange for you to come into the hospital. We, then, would have more
    time to talk about some of these issues and figure out in what ways we can
    be of help to you. How do you feel about that idea?
P: That's all right.
I: Good. I am going to have you wait outside while I do some of the
    paperwork. I enjoyed talking to you today and I want to thank you for
    allowing me to record the interview.
P: OK. Thank you (walking out).

III.D. A REPORT OF A PSYCHOLOGICAL EVALUATION

Mr. Smith is a 24-year-old single Black man who came by himself to the
emergency room of the hospital asking for help. The patient explained that
he had been "hearing people" tell him that he "must be a nut" and talked
about "strange" things happening to him, like feeling that others were making "notations" about him, or "changing the conversation" in a confusing and
ominous manner. Mr. Smith came to the Chicago area three months prior to
the evaluation and has reportedly been experiencing these problems for
three or four months.

Psychiatric History

Mr. Smith denied ever having emotional problems but apparently had
been admitted into a hospital several times while he was in the military

service. The impression was that these admissions were precipitated by psychiatric symptomatology. The patient was medicated during these admissions, but no further information was available about the treatment. He was able to recuperate to some degree, since he apparently finished his tour of duty in the military. Mr. Smith admitted smoking marijuana in the past but claimed not to have consumed any for the last four months. He denied the use of any other drugs. A history of psychiatric problems in the family was also denied.

Medical History

The medical history appeared to be noncontributory. A computed tomographic scan of the brain was apparently done during a previous hospitalization, but the results are unknown.

Family History

The patient was born and raised in Kansas, where his family still resides. The family consists of the two parents and two sisters, both younger than he. The patient joined the military to get away from conflictual family relationships.

Mr. Smith has been living by himself at the YMCA and is probably socially isolated.

Educational and Occupational History

After completing a high school education without any difficulties, the patient went into the Army. He was able to finish his four-year tour of duty but felt that some of his superiors did not want him; he apparently would not have been allowed to re-enlist. He was stationed in Michigan, where he stayed after his discharge from the military, attempting to obtain a job. He has been able to secure several temporary jobs but has been dismissed after an extremely brief period.

Mental Status

At the time of the interview Mr. Smith was alert, oriented, verbal, and coherent. Generally the intellectual and memory functions were intact, except that his response to proverbs was poor. The thought process was quite circumstantial and somewhat confused. The thought content was remarkable in the presence of paranoid delusions, probable auditory hallucinations, feelings of depersonalization, and delusions of reference. Projection was used frequently to deal with troublesome material, and Mr. Smith seemed to have no insight. An obsessive-compulsive defense (an emphasis on numbers and small details) was also seen. The affective response was a bit flat but was generally appropriate. The mood was within normal limits and showed a good range of emotions. No suicidal or homicidal ideation was expressed.

The psychomotor activity level and the anxiety level were within normal limits. The patient was friendly and cooperative. The only significant problem posed during the evaluation was that he was disorganized in his thinking, seemed defensive, and was not particularly well informed.

Assessment

Mr. Smith was actively psychotic at the time of the interview. The psychosis is mainly characterized by confusion and disorganization but includes vague persecutory delusions and probable auditory hallucinations. The symptomatology is likely to represent an acute exacerbation of a schizophrenic process that started several years ago while the patient was in active military service. The diagnosable problems appear to have followed a period of somewhat poor functioning when Mr. Smith was having considerable family problems.

Diagnostic Impressions

I. Schizophreniform disorder; rule out schizophrenia paranoid type
II. Obsessive-compulsive personality style
III. No known medical problems contributing

Recommendations

Admission into the psychiatric ward is recommended due to the patient's chronic disorganization and inability to care for himself. An evaluation for the use of psychotropic medications to reduce Mr. Smith's symptoms is indicated. Individual and group therapy should also be attempted. The patient's family should be contacted in order to discuss the possibility of Mr. Smith's return into their area.

IV Psychological Testing

IV.A. INTRODUCTION

Psychological testing involves three tasks: testing the patient, studying and interpreting the findings, and writing a report. How these tasks are done differs depending on the test and the purpose for the testing. This *Manual* will divide the subject matter into school, intellectual, emotional, and vocational evaluations.

Once the test is administered and scored in accordance with the rules offered in the appropriate test manual (e.g., the *WISC-R Manual* sold with the test), the scores can be interpreted. Interpretations of testing material (or other sources of information, for that matter) can be made at any of the following levels:

(a) Individual responses (e.g., the fact that the patient could not give the names of any past presidents of the United States on the WAIS-R can be taken as supporting the presence of a memory impairment).

(b) Test scores or group of individual responses (e.g., the low score obtained on Similarities in the WAIS-R can be interpreted as showing an inability to understand similarities and differences between objects).

(c) Strengths or problem areas (e.g., a patient may be seen as having difficulties with abstract thinking because he could not understand similarities and differences between objects, could not comprehend the meaning of particular social situations, and had trouble deducing a rule using a trial-and-error test).

(d) Profile or diagnostic formulation, representing a cluster of problem areas (e.g., the patient is thought to be schizophrenic because she showed poor contact with reality, had a paranoid delusion involving some of her co-workers, demonstrated a disorganized thought process, and was preoccupied with religious ideas).

(e) Etiological formulation or other interpretations made on the basis of assumptions related to the above profiles or cluster of problem areas (e.g., the patient developed an inadequate and avoidant personality disorder as a result of experiencing a rejecting father and an ineffective mother. This personality disorder prepared him very poorly for the demands of adult life, so that psychotic defenses had to be used when he was unable to separate from his family in his twenties.)

The further away an interpretation is from the actual data, the greater the chances that it is incorrect and the more tentative the psychologist must be in presenting it.

The information obtained from the testing is usually communicated by means of a psychological report. This report should be:

(a) Professional but also interesting and readable. Where the line is drawn between these two goals is a matter of personal judgment. Facts about the client's life, quotes from the client's responses, and changes in sentence structure should be used to make the report more meaningful and enjoyable. However, it is usually felt that jokes or extraneous anecdotes give an unprofessional flavor.

(b) The report should be well organized. Each paragraph should cover an easily identifiable issue. The shift from issue to issue should follow an organized plan.

(c) The report should be appropriate, containing all the information that can be useful but without burdening the reader with trivial details.

(d) Most psychological reports are written in the past tense. Although this rule is broken frequently enough, it remains a good rule to follow. This convention makes our reports read like the rest of the professional literature and reminds both the writer and the reader that it was written after seeing the client at a particular point in his or her life; human beings have a knack for changing, and statements that were true at one time may not be true at another.

(e) The issue of how much data should be given in support of interpretations or conclusions is highly contested. Some psychologists feel that it is unnecessary or even professionally incorrect to include the raw data or talk about the test findings themselves. As will be evident to the reader, I am most comfortable offering whatever information is available (at the risk of its being misinterpreted) and then making an effort to help those who have access to the report understand it and interpret it correctly. The data about the patient's background offered by most psychological reports is considerably briefer than the histories included in the examples given in this *Manual*. I believe in the usefulness of case reports that aspire to include all the relevant information about the subject. Even if it is unusual, this approach is followed here in order to give the reader more of a feeling for the patients about whom the reports were written, as well as a chance to see what such a comprehensive report may be like. This is one area, however, where the examples depart from what is most commonly done in our field. Reports that do not contain any of the test scores and that summarize the subject's background in a paragraph or two are much more typical.

The main traditionally used reference for reviews of psychological tests has been the *Mental Measurement Yearbook*. This work attempts to review every psychological test in the market, give information about the test's validity and reliability, update the available literature, and offer a critical evaluation of the test. Each issue of the *Yearbook* is meant to update the previous edition, so that a complete set is necessary. However, such sets are commonly available. The most recent update was edited by J. V. Mitchell. Other references are:

Keyser, D. J., & Sweetland, R. C. (Eds.). (1985-1986). *Test Critiques* (Vols. 1-4). Kansas City, MO: Test Corporation of America.
Sweetland, R. C., & Keyser, D. J. (Eds.). (1983). *Tests.* Kansas City, MO: Test Corporation of America.

IV.B. SCHOOL EVALUATIONS

School testing typically involves an intellectual evaluation with the goal of helping to design an appropriate educational program for a child. Although emotional evaluations are also commonly carried out in the educational system, this section will only cover cases in which the main issue is the child's intellectual functioning.

It is advisable to do an intellectual evaluation even when the complaint is behavioral, unless it is clear that the child does not have a learning or intellectual impairment. Children who have undiagnosed intellectual disabilities may find the school situation frustrating and may demonstrate nonadaptive behaviors as a result.

The subjects of these school evaluations are usually children who are not progressing with their school work at an acceptable pace (or who present behavioral problems, consistent with the above recommendation). The procedure to be followed usually involves:

(a) Becoming well informed about the difficulties that the child is having in the classroom, usually by discussing these issues with the school personnel.
(b) Obtaining background information about the child, either by becoming acquainted with social and health histories done by other school personnel or by directly interviewing a family member.
(c) Evaluating the child, usually by means of psychological tests.
(d) Writing a report.
(e) Participating in a multidisciplinary staffing where the findings will be integrated with those of other school personnel or consultants, a consensus of possible recommendations is arrived at, and both the evaluation and the recommendations are discussed with the parents.

The testing strategy usually consists of administering a general battery and later following up the low scores with other tests measuring functions similar to those in which the child did poorly. Typically the general battery includes an intelligence test (the Stanford-Binet, the Wechsler Preschool and Primary Scale of Intelligence, the revised Wechsler Intelligence Scale for Children, or the Kaufman Assessment Battery for Children) and a visuospatial task (Bender Gestalt or the Visual Motor Integration Test). In the absence of information from the school personnel regarding the pupil's academic level, an achievement test (e.g., the Peabody Individual Achievement Test, the revised Wide Range Achievement Test, or the achievement subtests from the KABC) should also be administered.

Table 6 presents a nonexhaustive list of school diagnoses and diagnostic indicators. Further help can be obtained from:

Bush, W. J., & Waugh, K. W. (1976). *Diagnosing learning disabilities.* Columbus, OH: Charles E. Merrill.
Kaufman, A. S. (1979). *Intelligent testing with the WISC-R.* New York: John Wiley & Sons.
Reynolds, C. R., & Gutkin, T. B. (1982). *The handbook of school psychology.* New York: John Wiley & Sons.
Sattler, J. M. (1988). *Assessment of children's intelligence* (3rd ed.). San Diego, CA: Jerome M. Sattler, Publisher.

The task of the multidisciplinary staff is to design the academic program that is best fitted for the particular student. At the low level of the "restrictive" or intensive spectrum are recommendations for the student, teachers, or parents for improving an area that is lagging behind while the child learns in the regular classroom. Ideas for such suggestions may be obtained from:

Blanco, R. G. (1972). *Prescriptions for children with learning and adjustment problems.* Springfield, IL: Charles C Thomas.

On the other hand, the multidisciplinary team may decide to recommend additional help. Typically the options available, in approximate order of restrictiveness, are:
   (a) The bilingual classroom (for children for whom English is not the native language).
   (b) The Title I Program, for children considered to have suffered from a substandard background.
   (c) The learning disability resource, in which the child is kept in the regular room except for a certain period during the day when tutorial help is offered.
   (d) Speech tutorial help.
   (e) Social work service for children with emotional, behavioral, or family problems.

TABLE 6. School Diagnoses and Diagnostic Indicators

Diagnosis	Function Impaired	IQ	Possible Diagnostic Indicators
Behavioral disorder	Emotional	80+	Rorschach, TAT, Children's Apperception Test, Blacky Pictures
Bilingualism	Language	80+	WISC-R Vocabulary ITPA Grammatic Closure, Auditory Closure, Verbal Expression KABC Expressive Vocabulary To lesser degree: WISC-R Comprehension, Information, Similarities; ITPA's auditory subtests
Cultural deprivation	Cultural knowledge	80+	WISC-R Comprehension, Information
Learning disability	Abstraction	80+	WISC-R Similarities, Comprehension ITPA Auditory Association, Visual Association KABC Matrix Analogies, Riddles
Learning disability	Attention	80+	WISC-R Arithmetic, Digit Span, Digit Symbol ITPA Visual Sequential Memory KABC sequential tasks
Language disability	Language	80+	WISC-R Vocabulary ITPA Grammatic Closure, Auditory Closure, Verbal Expression To lesser degree: WISC-R Comprehension, Information, Similarities; ITPA auditory subtests
Learning disability	Memory	80+	Wechsler Memory Scale, Benton Visual Retention Test
Learning disability	Sequential	80+	KABC sequential subtests WISC-R Digit Span, Picture Arrangement, Digit Symbol ITPA Auditory Sequential Memory, Visual Sequential Memory
Learning disability	Visualmotor	80+	Bender Gestalt, Visual Motor Integration Test WISC-R Coding, Mazes Frostig Test of Visual Perception
Learning disability	Visuospatial	80+	WISC-R Block Design, Object Assembly Raven's Progressive Matrices KABC simultaneous processing subtests
Speech impairment	Pronunciation		
Educable mental deficiency	All	55–80	All intellectual tests
Trainable mental deficiency	All intellectual	< 55	All intellectual tests

(f) A "developmental" classroom, a regular room designed for children who are behind and need to proceed at a slower pace. (This is considered a more restrictive program than the ones above because the child is expected to repeat the grade after finishing a year in the developmental room.)

(g) The learning disability classroom (LD) or self-contained placement, designed for students who have at least one area of intellectual deficiency but who demonstrate intactness in most other functions.

(h) The language learning disability (LLD) or communications disorder classroom, a specialized LD room for children with language learning disabilities.

(i) The behavioral disability classroom (BD), for children with emotional or discipline problems.

(j) The educable mentally handicap room (EMH), for children with low overall intellectual abilities.

(k) The trainable mentally handicap room (TMH), for children with very limited abilities.

Recommended Report Outline

(a) The referral problem: difficulties that the child has which have been previously noted; rationale for further assessment and the kind of information that is needed.

(b) Family history: parental sociocultural background; their social history prior to the present marriage; their age at the time of the marriage; their educational and occupational history; the siblings' names, ages, and activities; and the child's relationships in the family. (All of this information may be contained in a social history apart from the testing report.)

(c) Health history: difficulties with respect to the child during pregnancy or birth; medical problems or injuries sustained in the past. (This information may be contained in a health history apart from the testing report.)

(d) Developmental milestones: ages for the development of language, walking and motor abilities, toilet training, weaning, etc. (This information may be contained in a health history apart from the present report.)

(e) School history: list of all of the schools attended, the period of attendance, the levels of achievement, and any problems noted at earlier times.

(f) Behavioral observations: appearance (can be omitted when all readers know the child or when it is normal), description of examiner-client relationship, notable behaviors, motivation, attitudes toward testing, etc.

(g) Test scores.

(h) Discussion of test scores: general level of abilities, problems seen, intellectual strengths, the presence of any emotional issues that interfered with the child's ability to perform.

(i) Recommendations, which should include specific suggestions on how to improve any problems the child presents as well as the kind of setting that would best promote his or her progress. If a recommendation for placement is made, all of the options available in the particular school district should be kept in mind. The placement recommendation should be biased toward the less severe (least restrictive) alternative in cases in which some doubt exists.

Report Example

Referral Problem

John Fernandez is a 6-year-old Hispanic child who was referred for a psychological evaluation. According to the teacher's report, he is markedly behind the other first graders. He cannot count past the first few numbers, cannot copy his name, is very distractible, and has a very primitive vocabulary. The evaluation was requested in order to document his intellectual strengths and weaknesses and determine the best way to help him.

Family History

Mrs. Fernandez was interviewed as part of the evaluation. She is a 27-year-old Hispanic woman. Although she is overweight, she remains pleasant looking. She carried her youngest child, who is only 2 months old and who was asleep for most of the session. The examiner felt that she was at ease and related in an open manner with him, giving as much information as she could in response to questions.

Mrs. Fernandez was born in Mexico but immigrated to the United States when she was only 2 years old. She lived in Texas most of her life. At the age of 18, after finishing a grammar school education, she came to Illinois to live with her brother and sister-in-law. This home situation presented some problems, since Mrs. Fernandez felt that her sister-in-law did not like her and was constantly abusing her. As a result, when her first husband proposed to her, she accepted, even though she did not have much affection for him. They were quickly married, and John was conceived.

It was within the first year of the marriage that Mrs. Fernandez separated from her first husband. The incident that brought this about was the poor health of the child's maternal grandmother. The grandmother, who lived in

Texas, was diabetic, had become blind, and needed someone to care for her. Mrs. Fernandez's husband did not want to move and told Mrs. Fernandez that she had to choose between her mother and him. Mrs. Fernandez chose her mother and left. Although the mother died shortly thereafter, Mrs. Fernandez never returned and eventually filed for a divorce.

Three years later Mrs. Fernandez married her present husband. He is 39 years old. Although he was born in Texas, his family had originally come from Mexico. He was also married before and has four children from his previous marriage. He has little contact with these children. According to Mrs. Fernandez, she gets along well with her husband. He is very interested in the children and treats John like his own son.

There are two children who were born from this present marriage: Shirley is 4 and is presently attending kindergarten; Eddie is the 2-month-old baby.

Mrs. Fernandez does not know of any other member of the family who had severe difficulties in school. According to her, her daughter Shirley is doing well; however, the school already has expressed some concerns about her.

Mrs. Fernandez is not employed outside of the home. The family is maintained on Mr. Fernandez's income as a factory laborer. Although adequate, the income can allow only a very modest living style. Apparently both Mr. and Mrs. Fernandez are bilingual, and both Spanish and English are spoken at home. The mother feels that John can function better in Spanish than in English.

Health History

John was the product of an uncomplicated pregnancy. His birth, however, took place after 12 hours of labor and was the result of a cesarean section. John has not had serious medical problems but tends to get "bronchitis" or chest colds often.

A few years ago, when the family was still in Texas, it was thought that John was hyperactive. After a medical evaluation, he was put on an unknown medication that seemed effective in controlling his activity level. Last May, when the family moved to Illinois, the medication was discontinued. According to his mother, the hyperactivity has returned, but she is afraid of possible long-term effects of the medication and has chosen not to medicate him for the time being.

Developmental History

Mrs. Fernandez spoke with some feeling regarding John's difficulties in learning to talk. When he was 3 years old he was still not able to speak one single word. The mother blames herself for some of this retardation, since she used to get him what he wanted without forcing him to use a word to ask for it. Her second husband started to criticize her after a while for this attitude, and she then would force John to say the word "water" or whatever before she would get what he wanted. With that system he was able to learn the names of most common things. John, however, never uses sentences and tends to confine himself to simple nouns.

Mrs. Fernandez was also concerned about the way John relates to other children. She feels that he usually seeks kids who are older than he and sets up a relationship in which his friends physically abuse him. He never fights back and frequently comes home crying after being beaten up. Mrs. Fernandez has tried unsuccessfully to persuade John to find friends who are closer to his own age or, at least, to fight back. Her complaints to the parents of the older children have also been to no avail.

School History

John attended kindergarten at the Lincoln School in Chicago and has stayed there for his first grade. Last year John was reportedly at the bottom of the kindergarten group but the idea of referring him for an evaluation was not entertained. The higher demands of the first grade, however, have been taxing his ability to prosper, as already indicated.

Behavioral Observations

At first John was extremely shy even though he seemed comfortable with the examiner and did not show any signs of anxiety. He appeared to understand the examiner's Spanish throughout the testing but was extremely nonverbal, responding with his head whenever possible and verbalizing only single words. He knew a certain number of nouns but never used them in a sentence or even with articles or prepositions. Although some difficulties in pronunciation were noted, these difficulties seemed minor in the light of the primitive level of the language development.

John was also unable to understand instructions of any complexity. He was obedient and followed well any simple command. He was able to establish rapport with the examiner and responded very well to any kind of praise or encouragement. He was even able to relate well to playful interaction between the examiner and himself.

John was well dressed and seemed able to take care of his basic needs. John was able to sit on his chair for the first half-hour. After this time, an increasing level of activity was seen, but the hyperactivity was always of manageable proportions. The examiner could see, however, how this hyperactivity could be a little bit of a problem in the classroom situation, where he would have to spend more time and be more loosely controlled.

Test Results

Bender Gestalt: Five figures were administered. With the possible exception of the circle, the figures lost their gestalt so that they were completely unrecognizable. The quality of the drawings would place John at the bottom of the standardizing population.

Wechsler Intelligence Scale for Children, Revised (WISC-R)
(Unstandardized Spanish translation used)
Full Scale score = 45
Verbal Scale score = 45
Performance Scale score = 46
Information, scaled score = 0
Similarities = 4
Arithmetic = 0
Vocabulary = 0
Comprehension = 4
(Digit Span) = (1)
Picture Completion = 3
Picture Arrangement = 2
Block Design = 2
Object Assembly = 3
Coding = 1

Discussion

The test results indicate that John is functioning at a very low level. His highest scores (Similarities and Comprehension) do not suggest the presence of any higher abilities, since they are the result of his being able to answer only one test item correctly. There were, therefore, no signs in the tests administered of intellectual abilities approximating the average range in any of the areas tested. The low achievement scores are also consistent with low generalized intellectual functioning.

The test findings are supported by the child's history. The retardation of the language development was very extreme and goes along with a severe level of intellectual impairment. Moreover, the other problems, like the peculiar relationship with other children, may also be reflecting his low level of intellectual abilities. It is possible that the problems seen were caused by the long labor and birth trauma, since no other medical problems or accidents were uncovered during the evaluation. The presence of mild hyperactivity could be seen as consistent with an organic condition.

The family history revealed some problems in the past (the parental separation and divorce, the move to Texas and back, and the entry of the new stepfather into the family). The educational and financial resources of the family are also somewhat limited. However, the family system appears to be more stable at this time, and none of these factors could explain the kind of intellectual deficits seen during the testing. It was felt, as a result, that if the family background presented problems, they were probably minor when contrasted to the intellectual impairment.

Conclusions and Recommendations

On the basis of the present evaluation, John would be seen as functioning at a very low level and needing intensive individualized help if he is to obtain any benefits from his educational program. If there is any doubt about his limited abilities, an Adaptive Behavior Scale may be completed by having the mother rate John's abilities in the home in the different areas included in this scale. However, it was obvious during the interview with the mother that he was functioning very poorly at home as well. When considering the option of a special education placement in the multidisciplinary staffing, it should be kept in mind that John has no physical disabilities, has mastered the hygiene and primary care training, and is able to communicate emotionally with others.

The following specific recommendations may also be considered:

1. Training in basic communication skills. Included here would be improving vocabulary, learning the use of numbers, and perhaps learning to form some sentences.

2. Training in living skills, such as the use of money, the recognition of coins of different denominations, the use of a clock, and the concept of time.

3. Help in social skills. As is often the case with individuals of his intellectual level, John apparently tends to feel inadequate with other children and to be abused by them. Teaching of appropriate behaviors with other children would be very beneficial.

4. Helping the Fernandez family accept and adjust to John's limitations. Although the frustration and protectionism of Mrs. Fernandez is understandable, the stepfather could be an ally in helping John to behave in the most appropriate manner of which he is capable.

Since children with moderate and severe intellectual impairments often have neurological abnormalities, and since John was the product of a possibly traumatic birth and has received psychotropic medications in the past, the examiner would strongly recommend a neurological workup. At the very least, a neurologist could evaluate the need for further medication. Ruling out the presence of an active and treatable neurological disorder seems also of primary importance.

In terms of long-term goals, the examiner would recommend that a psychological reevaluation be undertaken every few years in order to assess any progress that is made. Good vocational training in the future would also seem of great importance.

IV.C. INTELLECTUAL EVALUATION OF ADULTS

The use of psychological testing for assessing a person's intellectual functioning has increasingly evolved into the field of neuropsychology, especially in the case of adults. This trend has been fueled by the interest on the part of psychologists in correlating their findings with the neurological or medical results. The trend has also been a response to the limitations imposed on intellectual evaluations if these evaluations involve only the measurement of abilities without any further understanding.

The relationship between neuropathology and intellectual impairment is not one to one. Many individuals who have a neurological disorder do not show any intellectual impairment, and some intellectual deficits may be due to a lack of the normally distributed innate ability and may have no relationship to brain damage. Often, however, substantial intellectual deficits, especially those acquired in adulthood, are due to neuropathology.

A good way to organize the material in this area is to think of the brain as a refined computer. Three operations may be distinguished: the input, the process, and the output.

The input may be external or internal and includes a perception of the organism's own behaviors. The external input involves the stimulation of some receptor (e.g., the eye), the transmission of the stimulus through nerves, and the activation of some part of the central nervous system. The visual area is located in the occipital cortex, the auditory in the temporal lobe, and the tactile and kinesthetic in the postcentral gyrus. Studies by Hubel and Wiesel (1962) found the cortex to be further organized into three levels as it goes deeper into the brain. The primary or surface level serves as a screen onto which the stimulus is projected. The secondary and tertiary levels function by grouping the stimulus in a way that allows the organism to "synthesize" or "understand" the information received. For instance, stimulation of the primary visual cortex may lead to the perception of a flash of light; stimulation of the secondary and tertiary zones may lead to the perception of images of objects or familiar persons that are seen in a moving, meaningful, and dynamic way. Table 7 reviews the main input functions of the brain, diagnosable disorders involving those functions, the possible brain location of damaged tissue, and some suggestions for methods of evaluation.

The processing operation involves:

(a) A "plan of attack," which includes an understanding of what has to be accomplished and the organization of the organism toward the goal-directed behavior of accomplishing the given task.

TABLE 7. Main Input Functions of the Brain

Function	Possible Disorders	Brain Locations	Suggested Method of Evaluation
Attention	Inability to concentrate on incoming stimuli	Hypocampus; amygdala	
SENSATION			
Visual	Loss of part of visual field	Occipital lobe	Neurological exam
	Unawareness of one side of visual field	Contralateral parieto-temporal	Bender Gestalt
Auditory	Reduction of auditory acuity	Lateral temporal	Neurological exam
Tactile	Loss of sensation in some part of body	Contralateral postcentral gyrus	Neurological exam
Kinesthetic	Afferent paresis: inability to control gross movement due to lack of kinesthetic input	Contralateral postcentral gyrus	Neurological exam
	Afferent motor aphasia: difficulty in articulation due to lack of kinesthetic input	Dominant postcentral gyrus	

(b) A search for the needed information, representing a control of the input activities by the processing operation.

(c) Perception, or interpretative integration of the input.

(d) Memory, or interpretative integration of the present input with past experiences.

(e) Cognition, or the ability to go beyond the concrete input and make abstract interpretations.

The frontal lobes play the very important function of organizing behavior so that the person performs in a goal-directed way. The rest of the process functions are carried on generally by the secondary and tertiary levels of the cortex. Mode specificity is present: for instance, the formation of visual images associated with spoken words relies on the temporo-occipital cortex, which is thought to integrate the verbal modality based in the temporal lobe with the visual modality of the occipital lobe. Table 8 reviews the information pertaining to the process operation of the brain.

The output operation consists of movement, which includes speech, and relies on the frontal lobe's organizational capacity and the movement functions of the precentral gyri. Further information is given in Table 9.

TABLE 8. Main Process Functions of the Brain

Function	Possible Disorders	Brain Locations	Suggested Method of Evaluation
Planning	Inability to function in a purposeful manner	Frontal lobes	Wechsler's Picture Arrangement Arithmetic Category Test Wisconsin Card Sort
Tracking	Inability to shift attention from one incoming stimulus to another	Frontal lobes	Wechsler's Digit Symbol Trail Making Test
PERCEPTION			
Visual	Optic agnosia: inability to synthesize elements of objects into recognizable wholes	ND—parieto-occipital	Bender Gestalt Hooper Visual Organization Test
	Simultaneous agnosia: inability to perceive more than one object at one time	ND—parieto-occipital	
	Optic alexia: inability to perceive letters	D—parieto-occipital	Aphasia Screening Test
	Inability to form visual image associated with word	D—temporo-occipital	Aphasia Screening Test
Auditory	Acoustic agnosia or sensory aphasia: inability to synthesize auditory stimuli into a recognizable whole (receptive language capacity)	D—temporal	Aphasia Screening Test
	Sensory amusia: inability to synthesize rhythms or sounds	ND—temporal	Seashore Rhythm Test
Tactile	Astereognosis: inability to synthesize tactile stimuli into a recognizable whole	D—parietal	Rey's Skin Writing Test

TABLE 8. *(continued)*

Function	Possible Disorders	Brain Locations	Suggested Method of Evaluation
Kinesthetic	Disturbed body scheme or perception of body (usually leads to dressing apraxia or difficulty in dressing)	ND—parietal	Neurological exam
	Afferent apraxia: inability to synthesize kinesthetic input leading to disturbance of fine motor movement	Postcentral gyrus	Neurological exam
	Anosognosia: inability to recognize own defects or errors	ND—parietal	
Memory	Amnesic aphasia: inability to recall names	D—temporal	Aphasia Screening Test
	Optic aphasia: inability to recall visual images in response to spoken words (i.e., draw figure of object named)	D—temporo-occipital	Aphasia Screening Test
	Acoustic amnesia: disturbance of audio-verbal memory	D—temporal	Wechsler Memory Scale
	Disturbance of spatial memory	D—parieto-occipital	Benton Visual Retention Test Wechsler Memory Scale
Cognition	Spatial disorientation: inability to find bearings in spatial coordinates	D—parieto-occipital	Trail Making Test
	Construction apraxia: inability to understand spatial designs	D—parieto-occipital	Wechsler's Block Design Object Assembly
	Inability to understand logical-grammatical relationships	D—parieto-occipital	Wechsler's Arithmetic Similarities

D = dominant hemisphere; ND = nondominant hemisphere

It should be obvious that one cannot test one operation in isolation. Any task that the organism is asked to perform will involve input, processing, and output. A particular task, however, may involve a high level of difficulty in only one of the operations. For instance, the question "How are a pear and an apple alike?" involves a relatively easy input and output but is thought to test the thinking capacity of the organism. However, the diagnostician always has to keep in mind that, if the stimulus is not heard and perceived appropriately, the assumption that a particular question taps the thinking capacity may be erroneous.

Lewis and Swiercinsky (1981) suggested that appropriate referrals for neuropsychological evaluations usually involve one of the following goals:

(a) To demonstrate intellectual deficits in an individual suspected of organicity.

(b) To assess the effects of a known lesion or dysfunction on the patient's ability to function.

(c) To help plan appropriate treatment or remediation of an intellectual deficiency.

(d) To establish an objective baseline in order to monitor the effects of treatment or the course of the illness.

(e) To better understand the patient's intellectual strengths and deficits.

A comprehensive neuropsychological evaluation involves testing the different parts of the system in an attempt to determine the nature of any deficiency.

TABLE 9. Main Output Functions of the Brain

Function	Possible Disorders	Brain Location	Suggested Method of Evaluation
Movement	Inability to move in a smooth and integrated manner	Precentral gyrus	Neurological exam Finger Tapping Test
Speech	Inability to flow from one sound to the next (one single sound presents no problem regardless of sound)	Precentral gyrus	Aphasia Screening Test
	Word substitution with incorrect but better-known words	Frontal lobes	
	Broca's aphasia: difficulty in organizing words into meaningful speech	D—temporal	

D = dominant hemisphere

The basic premise is that any intellectual function can be impaired as the result of organic damage. As much as the functions of the different parts of the brain are known, once the existence of a particular deficiency has been established, it is sometimes possible to pinpoint the location of the damage.

The comprehensive neuropsychological evaluation is best accomplished through the use of a test battery that systematically assesses the different functions. There are two well-known batteries in existence. The older is the Halstead-Reitan Neuropsychological Battery. The newer Luria-Nebraska Neuropsychological Battery has a better conceptualized theoretical basis, but it has considerably less research support at this time. Many neuropsychologists, however, do not use either of the batteries in their entirety but have a much briefer starting battery of their own. The strategy is to get a preliminary sampling of functions with the mini-battery and then go from there, testing further the specific functions involved in the presenting complaint or the functions that seem to be deficient. A common starting battery for adults includes the Wechsler Adult Intelligence Scale (WAIS), the Wechsler Memory Scale, and the Halstead Aphasia Screening Test.

The Halstead-Reitan Neuropsychological Battery includes, in addition to the Wechsler Adult Intelligence Scale and the Minnesota Multiphasic Personality Inventory (MMPI), the following tests:

(a) Aphasia Screening Test. The test involves naming, reading, spelling, drawing geometric figures, repeating hard-to-pronounce phrases, and following a simple command. Tapping a variety of expressive and receptive language abilities, this screening instrument is also useful in the evaluation of agnosia and apraxia.

(b) Halstead Category Test. In its original form, this test consists of 208 slides containing mainly geometric figures, each of which is associated in some manner with the number 1, 2, 3, or 4. It is the subject's task to figure out what the correct response is through trial and error. Presently there are a booklet, a card, a short version, and several computer versions of this test at different stages of validation. The test is thought to measure abstract reasoning, planning and tracking abilities, memory, and learning speed.

(c) Trail Making Test. The trails require the subject to connect circles in order, first following numbers only (Part A), and then alternating numbers and letters (Part B). The test is thought to measure planning and tracking abilities and motor speed.

(d) Tactual Performance Test (TPT). This test consists of a form board that has ten holes with different geometric shapes. The task is to place wooden blocks in the correct holes while blindfolded. The test employs tactile and kinesthetic abilities and is a good indicator of lateralized functioning of the sensory strip in the cortex.

(e) Seashore Rhythm Test. This test requires the subject to determine if two different recorded rhythms are the same or different. The task is thought to measure a nondominant hemisphere function.

(f) Speech Sounds Perception Test. This test requires the subject to match prerecorded nonsense words with a multiple choice of printed words. The task involves accurate translation of sound perceptions into written language.

(g) Finger Tapping Test (FTT) (also called the Finger Oscillation Test). Measures the speed of tapping with the index finger of both hands and is thought to be a good indicator of lateralized cortical functioning of the motor strip area.

(h) Sensory Perceptual Examination. This test involves the presentation of auditory stimuli, fingertip number writing, finger identification, and tactile form recognition. It is designed to evaluate the accuracy of the patient's sensory-perceptual system.

(i) Lateral Dominance Examination. This task involves asking the patient if he or she would prefer to use the right or the left extremities in carrying out a number of different activities.

The Luria-Nebraska Neuropsychological Battery was developed by Charles J. Golden at the University of Nebraska (Golden, 1985). The battery is designed as a thorough and standardized mental status examination following the suggestions generated by Luria's work in Russia. The battery consists of eleven sections that test Motor, Rhythm and Pitch, Tactile, Visual, Receptive Language, Writing, Reading, Arithmetic, Memory, and Intellectual skills.

The "screening" approach is a less sophisticated way of evaluating individuals for possible neurological deficits. The theory that all individuals with organic brain syndromes will respond in a similar way to psychological tests has long been rejected. It is now known that the functions impaired differ from one individual to another and are related to the location and the extent of the damaged tissue, as well as the amount of time since the damage took place. Nevertheless, it is also true that some functions are more prone to impairment in individuals with organic brain damage than are others. This fact makes it possible to use, for screening purposes, an instrument that taps a limited number of functions and can be administered quickly. The screening approach is particularly useful when a large number of individuals have to be evaluated. There are several screening instruments on the market, with differing degrees of complexity. Some of the single-task instruments are so effective, however, that their accuracy is not easily surpassed. Recommended instruments are:

(a) The Halstead Category Test, which has been shown to predict correctly 94% of the brain damaged (Shaw, 1966). However, in my experience, it diagnoses as brain damaged many individuals who are not.

(b) The Trail Making Test has been also shown to discriminate effectively between the normal population and individuals known to have organic damage (Reitan, 1958).

It is important to note that all the neuropsychological tests, and especially the screening instruments, lose substantial accuracy when the task is to discriminate between organic and psychiatric patients.

The most defensible way of diagnosing organicity is by comparing premorbid and postmorbid test scores. Any significant drop in scores measuring a particular function beyond what is expected as a result of aging presumably would be due to an organic impairment. However, seldom does the examiner have the advantage of available premorbid scores. In most cases the examiner has to estimate the original level of ability. This estimate is made by looking at the individual's higher (and presumable unimpaired) scores, by considering scores on tasks that tend to be resistant to the effects of organicity (e.g., Wechsler's Vocabulary), and by using the client's history. In the historical data, of particular interest are the amount of schooling completed, how well the person did in school, and his or her occupational history. Low scores are then evaluated in light of this estimated premorbid ability.

Neurological diagnostic accuracy has been greatly improved by such recent developments as the electroencephalogram and the computer-assisted brain scan techniques. As a result, the emphasis in neuropsychology probably will shift away from the diagnosis and localization of brain damage to determining the areas of difficulty so that remediation can be planned and an accurate assessment of the client's handicap can be made possible.

Neuropsychology aims to study a very complex system. Caution must be exercised so that we, as practitioners, do not make claims that go beyond the state of the art. In doing this type of work or looking at the neuropsychological literature, one is impressed by how individuals who supposedly have the same kind of brain lesion show very different test performance. Some of these differences may be explained in terms of the premorbid abilities, since all of our clients did not start at the same place intellectually. Moreover, the accepted relationships between different areas of the brain and the intellectual functions (such as those we have reported) are sometimes based on a small number of cases and should be seen as tentative. More than in any of the other areas covered in this *Manual,* readers should be advised to seek good supervision before accepting the simplistic and superficial information offered here.

The following books are recommended for further reading:

Filskov, S. B., & Boll, T. J. (Eds.). (1981, 1986). *Handbook of clinical neuropsychology* (Vols. 1 & 2). New York: John Wiley & Sons. (A comprehensive review of neuropsychology.)

Gardner, E. (1975). *Fundamentals of neurology: A psychophysiological approach.* Philadelphia: Saunders. (This book offers background in understanding the functioning of the neuron and the basic structuring of the nervous system.)

Hynd, G., & Obrzut, J. E. (Eds.). (1981). *Neuropsychological assessment of the school-aged child: Issues and procedures.* Orlando, FL: Grune & Stratton.

Jarvis, P. E., & Barth, J. T. (1984). *The Halstead-Reitan Test Battery: An interpretative guide.* Odessa, FL: Psychological Assessment Resources. (A good brief review of the Halstead-Reitan Battery.)

Lezak, M. D. (1983). *Neuropsychological assessment* (2nd ed.). New York: Oxford University Press. (This work is a very useful discussion of the different neuro-psychological tests, how they are used, and what the different tests are thought to measure.)

Luria, A. R. (1973). *The working brain: An introduction to neuropsychology.* New York: Basic Books. (A discussion by this Russian pioneer of the behavioral effects of lesions in the different areas of the cortex.)

Reitan, R. M., & Wolfson, D. (1985). *The Halstead-Reitan Neuropsychological Test Battery.* Tucson, AZ: Neuropsychology Press. (This work contains many valuable case reports.)

Reitan, R. M., & Wolfson, D. (1985). *Neuroanatomy and neuropathology: A clinical guide for neuropsychologists.* Tucson, AZ: Neuropsychology Press.

Reitan, R. M., & Wolfson, D. (1985). *Traumatic brain injury: Pathophysiology and neuropsychological evaluation.* Tucson, AZ: Neuropsychology Press.

Strub, R. L., & Black, F. W. (1981). *Organic brain syndromes.* Philadelphia: F. A. Davis. (Provides a good review of the major disease entities involving cortical functioning, such as the dementias, closed head trauma, etc.)

Recommended Report Outline

  (a) The referral question (what problems have been noted, the rationale for further assessment, and the kind of information needed)
  (b) Psychiatric history
  (c) Medical history
  (d) Family history
  (e) Educational and occupational history
  (f) Mental status and behavioral observations made during the testing
  (g) Test results
  (h) Discussion or interpretation of the test results, which may include:
    i. A statement giving the current overall ability.
    ii. A statement about how the current ability may compare to the subject's premorbid functioning.
    iii. What specific functions are deficient, and how deficient these functions currently appear.
    iv. A discussion of the diagnostic picture that emerges and how this picture may fit the neurological information available.
    v. What can be said about the prognosis.

(i) Diagnostic formulation
(j) Recommendations, in which the following should be taken into account:
   i. In cases where the deterioration is severe, the need for placement has to be addressed.
   ii. When the patient has not been seen by a neurologist and an organic involvement appears probable, a neurological work-up should be recommended.
   iii. Recommendations for remediation.
   iv. Recommendations regarding how to deal with problems that may not be improved.

Report Example

Mr. Frank Memor is an 85-year-old white man who was alleged to be incompetent to handle his financial affairs. The present evaluation was conducted at the request of his daughter and her lawyer in order to document any intellectual deficiencies that he may have.

When asked if he was experiencing any problems with his mental functioning, Mr. Memor stated that he had become very "forgetful" and that he was often "puzzled" by the situation he was facing.

The evaluation consisted of an interview and the administration of most of the Halstead-Reitan Neuropsychological Battery. The patient was accompanied by his daughter, Mrs. Dorothy Haber, who helped the patient furnish the historical information.

Psychiatric History

Mr. Memor has never had any emotional problems and has never been a substance abuser. The family history revealed no psychiatric disorders.

Medical History

Mr. Memor had a double hernia repair in 1966 and was hospitalized with shingles in 1974. Last February he was admitted into Jackson Memorial Hospital for testing. The family was reportedly told that he had vascular problems leading to diminished oxygen supply to his heart and brain. The physician, Dr. Albert Gasser, told Mr. Memor that he should no longer drive. The only other notable medical event was a hospitalization at Jackson Memorial for pneumonia a month ago.

Family History

Mr. Memor was born and raised in Washington, D.C., the oldest of four siblings. Both of the parents died at an elderly age when the patient was already in his sixties. The father had maintained the family through a gas station that he owned and operated; the mother was a housewife.

Mr. Memor was widowed three years ago after fifty-eight years of marriage. The marriage was the first for both him and his wife. He was able to express the sorrow he had felt at the loss of his wife but seemed to have worked through his period of bereavement by now.

The patient has five children, all of whom are alive and well. James (56) is married, has six children of his own, and works as a car mechanic. Frank Jr. (54) drives a truck for a delivery service. He is married and has three children. Married, with one child, and living in Colorado is Jean (53). Following the family traditional occupation—owning a gas station—is Paul (52). He is married, has three children, and lives in Kansas City. Dorothy (48) is the youngest member of the family. She is married and has four children.

Mr. Memor is presently living by himself in the house into which he moved seventeen years ago. He has a grandson who stays with him several nights a week in order to make sure that he is all right. He also has a son who comes into the area twice a week and stays with Mr. Memor on those days. This arrangement has apparently provided adequate checks so that there have been no significant problems with his capacity to deal with his daily living.

Educational History

Mr. Memor obtained his high school diploma from Burbank Academy when this school was located in Washington. He was an excellent student and remembered graduating among the top four students in his class.

Occupational History

Together with one of his brothers, Mr. Memor owned and operated two gas stations from 1930 until 1967. For the thirteen years that followed, he continued to do some work at the gas station that one of his sons owned. Thus, it has been only in the past six or seven years that he has been fully retired.

Mental Status Examination

At the time of the evaluation the patient was alert, oriented, verbal, and coherent. Speech and language functions were intact. Mr. Memor was unable to recall many of the dates of important events in his life, especially those in his recent past. For instance, he was unable to say when his wife died, how many years he had lived at his present residence, and the like. He often confused the names of his grandchildren, ascribing to one family a grandchild that actually belonged to another family. Other intellectual functions were formerly examined and will be discussed below. The thought process was orderly but confused. The patient was unable, for instance, to understand the reason why he was being examined and stated that he would refuse to go to court because he "had not committed any crime." This statement was made after the examiner explained that some members of his family felt that he needed help in managing his money. The test instructions often had to be repeated several times before the patient was able to understand what was expected of him. The thought content was normal. The affective response was always appropriate. The mood was within normal limits and demonstrated a good range of emotions. There was no suicidal or homicidal ideation. Psychomotor activity and anxiety levels were within normal limits. Mr. Memor was friendly and cooperative throughout the morning.

Test Results

Aphasia Screening Test
  No problems were found.

Wechsler Adult Intelligence Scale—Revised (WAIS-R)
  Verbal Scale IQ = 97
  Performance Scale IQ = 82
  Full Scale IQ = 88
  Information, scaled score = 6
  Digit Span = 9
  Vocabulary = 10
  Arithmetic = 7
  Similarities = 5
  Picture Completion = 5
  Picture Arrangement = 5
  Block Design = 3
  Object Assembly = 2
  Digit Symbol = 2

Wechsler Memory Scale
  Information = 3
  Orientation = 2
  Mental Control = 9
  Memory Passages = 5
  Digits total = 10
  Visual Reproduction = 3
  Pair Associate Learning = 8
  Memory Quotient = 100

Russell Adaptation of Wechsler Memory Scale
  (30' delayed recall)
  Memory Passages = 0
  Visual Reproductions = 0

Finger Tapping Test
  Average, dominant hand = 48
  Average, nondominant hand = 36

Trail Making Test
  Time, Trail A = 1' 40"
  Time, Trail B = 4' 30"

Discussion

Doing an intellectual evaluation with an 85-year-old person presents a problem in that the psychological tests available often do not offer norms for people of that age. The WAIS-R is undoubtedly the best and more thoroughly standardized instrument of its kind, and its norms go up only to the age of 74 years. What is normally done to cope with this deficiency is to use interpolation, estimating what the score may be by extending the normative curve derived from testing younger individuals. This method assumes that the intellectual losses normally suffered, say, during the years 60 through 74 will be similar to what is normally lost from the time the person is 74 years old until he or she is, for instance, 88. Even though this method is the best that can be done at this time, it clearly is based on questionable assumptions, since it uses as its basis for prediction the years during which individuals are known to lose a significant amount of their intellectual capacity.

Many of the scores just reported were derived using the procedure described and should be seen as rough estimates of how Mr. Memor would compare to his age peers. These scores suggest that the patient has verbal abilities as good as those of most people his age. This was apparently known to the patient and his daughter, since they were not surprised by the finding. It is this good verbal ability that allows the patient to carry on a reasonable conversation with another individual and make a good first impression.

The memory capacity is the function that Mr. Memor's daughter and even Mr. Memor himself complained about. The memory function is especially susceptible to aging, so that much is lost even during the earlier years of older adulthood. When the Wechsler Memory Scale was given to Mr. Memor, the score obtained using the procedure noted was actually within the normal range for a person of his age. Since this test measures immediate recall or short-term memory, the finding suggested that Mr. Memor is able to code new information as well as can be expected.

The Russell Adaptation of the Wechsler Memory Scale was performed. The procedure calls for recall of some of the learned material thirty minutes after it was originally given. In contrast to most of the other tests used, norms with an elderly population are available for the Russell Adaptation. Mr. Memor was unfortunately unable to recall any of the information involved, a performance that was substantially below what was expected according to the norms. Thus, even though Mr. Memor is able to code new information, the data showed that he loses the memory trace so that, after thirty minutes have elapsed, he cannot even remember having been given the material to memorize.

Unfortunately, long-term memory also left something to be desired. For instance, Mr. Memor had difficulty remembering important dates such as when his wife died, the zip code of an address at which he has lived for 17 years, or how much younger than he is his younger sister. He had significant difficulty with the names and clustering of his grandchildren and often gave erroneous information.

There were additional areas in which Mr. Memor did not perform as well as would have been expected using the derived normative estimates. One such area was mental flexibility (Digit Symbol and Trail Making Test) and abstractions (Similarities). These deficits speak to his complaint that he is "puzzled" by different situations that he faces, since it would lead to an inability to keep the major elements of a situation in mind at the same time and would result in difficulty conceptualizing the meaning of the situation.

Also deficient but not related to any of the presenting complaints was visuospatial functioning. This impairment was indicated by a Performance Scale score 15 points lower than that on the Verbal Scale. The finding suggested that Mr. Memor would have more difficulty than most of the people of his age in understanding the placement of objects in space, remembering directions in order to go from one place to another, following a map, and the like.

The visuospatial deficit is probably inconsequential in regard to Mr. Memor's ability to take care of his financial affairs. The impairment of the recent memory, his inability to keep track of information, and his incapacity to conceptualize abstractions, however, are very serious impairments. It is my opinion that, given these deficits, Mr. Memor would not be able to handle his financial affairs effectively.

Diagnostic Impressions

I—Dementia
II—Personality diagnosis deferred
III—No known medical problems contributing

IV.D. TESTING FOR PSYCHODYNAMICS

A good evaluation of psychodynamics cannot be done without thorough knowledge of the patient's history. A "blind" interpretation of personality tests is an interesting academic exercise but makes many of the test results hard to interpret and precludes integration of test findings with the history. In clinical situations, it needlessly places the examiner at a disadvantage. As a result, if a good history is not already available, the examiner is encouraged to do a thorough interview at the beginning of the evaluation (see Chapter III for details).

The emotional make-up of a person leaves an imprint on anything that the person does. One could obtain, for instance, much useful data from watching a group of patients play a competitive table game. The information that follows, however, will be restricted to tests that were especially designed as psychodiagnostic tools.

Personality tests are of two types: personality inventories and projective techniques. Personality inventories are standardized questionnaires that the subject answers alone. Table 10 gives information about the commonly used personality inventories. These tests have the advantage of not taking much of the examiner's time, being able to be used by examiners with little training, and having relatively high validity and reliability. Their disadvantages are that, since they are much more structured than the projective techniques, the amount of information that they give is more limited: they tend to force the subjects into molds, they rely on the subjects' ability to perceive themselves accurately, and they rely on the subjects' willingness to share their own self-images nondefensively.

Projective techniques, on the other hand, are fairly unstructured: the subject is given some brief instructions and then is encouraged to give material that is later interpreted. Table 11 gives information about the projective techniques that are commonly used. Projective techniques require much training and take considerable time to administer, and interpretations are much more subjective than they are with the inventories. Nevertheless, in the hands of a capable examiner, they can yield many useful insights about the subject.

Recommended Report Outline

(a) The referral question
    i. Problems already noted
    ii. Rationale for further evaluation
    iii. Type of information sought
(b) Family history (optional; often omitted)
    i. Ethnic and socioeconomic status of family of origin
    ii. Brief description of members of the family

TABLE 10. Commonly Used Personality Inventories

Name	Scoring	Major Areas Evaluated
California Personality Inventory	Auto & manual	480 items measuring poise, ascendancy, self-assurance, adequacy, socialization, responsibility, intrapersonal values, character, achievement, potential, intellectual efficiency, and interests. Reference: Megargee, 1972
Edwards Personality Inventory	Auto & manual	225 items measuring achievement, deference, order, exhibition, autonomy, affiliation, intraception, succorance, dominance, abasement, nurturance, change, endurance, heterosexuality, and aggression.
Millon Clinical Multiaxial Inventory (MCMI)	Auto & manual	175 items measuring the 8 Millon personality styles, deteriorations of the basic personality (schizotypal, cycloid, and paraphrenic), as well as 9 symptom clusters (anxiety, somatic preoccupations, hypomania, dysthymia, alcohol abuse, drug abuse, psychotic thinking, psychotic depression, and psychotic delusion). Reference: Millon, 1969
Millon Adolescent Personality Inventory (MAPI)	Auto	150 items meant for use with adolescents. Besides the 8 personality styles, the test taps concerns regarding self-concept, personal esteem, body comfort, sexual acceptance, family rapport, and academic confidence; and behavioral correlates such as impulse control, social conformity, scholastic achievement, and attendance constancy.
Millon Behavioral Health Inventory (MBHI)	Auto	150 items designed for medical patients. Besides the 8 personality styles, the test measures psychogenic issues such as chronic tension, recent stress, premorbid pessimism, future despair, social alienation, and somatic anxiety. Psychosomatic inclinations (allergic, gastrointestinal, and cardiovascular) and prognostic measures (pain treatment responsivity, life-threat reactivity, and emotional vulnerability) are also obtained.
Minnesota Multiphasic Personality Inventory (MMPI)	Auto & manual	566 items measuring validity of results and hypochondriasis, depression, hysterical tendencies, psychopathy, gender identity, paranoia, psychasthenia, schizophrenia, hypomania, and social introversion. There is also a multitude of experimental scales. References: Graham, 1987; Greene, 1980; Lachar, 1974; Marks, Seeman, & Haller, 1974
Sixteen Personality Factors (16PF)	Auto & manual	187 items measuring 16 interpersonal trait continua such as reserved vs. outgoing, practical vs. imaginative, dependent vs. self-sufficient.

TABLE 11. Commonly Used Projective Techniques

Name	Major Areas Evaluated	References
Bender Gestalt	View of the self	Hutt, 1985
(Hutt Adaptation)	Dynamic issues	Koppitz, 1963
	Psychopathology	
Draw-a-Person	View of self and	Koppitz, 1967, 1984
	members of oppo-	Oster & Gould, 1987
	site sex	
Family drawings	View of self and	
	meaningful others	
Rorschach	Personality style	Aronow & Reznikoff, 1976
Inkblot Test	Dynamic issues	Beck et al., 1961
	Psychopathology	Klopfer et al., 1954
		Exner, 1974, 1978
		Exner & Weiner, 1982
Thematic	Personality style	Bellak, 1986
Apperception	Dynamic issues	Tomkins, 1947
Test	Interpersonal relations	

  iii. Brief description of the manner in which the patient relates to significant family members
  iv. Important events that took place during childhood
  v. Description of the present family if it is not the family of origin
  vi. Description of the relationship between the patient and the present family members
  vii. Important events that have taken place in the present family
  viii. Important social relationships outside the family
 (c) Educational and occupational history (often omitted)
  i. Extent of the education received
  ii. Types and period of employment
 (d) Behavioral observations
  i. Appearance
  ii. Description of patient-examiner interactions
  iii. General behaviors (personal comments made by the patient, unusual behaviors, etc.)
  iv. Specific test behaviors (motivation, defensiveness, attitudes toward testing, etc.)
 (e) Tests administered (occasionally the test scores are also included in this section)
 (f) Discussion (see further explanation following outline)
 (g) Recommendations

    i. Suggestions of changes in the environment that would decrease the amount of stress

   iii. Suggestions of changes in the psychic process that would make the individual better able to cope with the world

   iii. Concrete ways of achieving these changes

   iv. No recommendation should be made when the purpose of the evaluation was simply to gain more information

   v. No recommendation should be made in areas where the examiner is not qualified (e.g., type of medication)

(h) Summary

Of all the sections of a psychological report, the discussion probably allows the best expression of the examiner's creativity and originality. More so than any other part of the report, this section allows the examiner to draw a picture for the reader of what the patient is all about: the client's psychological essence and the reason the client is experiencing whatever problems are present. It is in the discussion section that all the data are integrated and interpreted so as to psychologically distinguish that person from the rest of humanity. The opportunity to be creative and imaginative, however, carries with it the difficulty of having to organize all the information available about the subject and interpret it in a way that is revealing, meaningful, and appropriate. As a result, it is in this section that the writings of the unexperienced are most easily distinguished from those of an accomplished professional.

Common errors made by the beginner in the discussion section are the following:

(a) Presenting the material without a theme to link it together.

(b) Having a series of unrelated statements about the client in the same paragraph.

(c) Having statements that read like the testing text books or manuals rather than like a genuine description of a unique person.

(d) Lacking the right balance between giving no factual support for the statements made (and thus sounding as if one developed a series of subjective opinions about the patient), and giving so much support that one ends up talking about the psychological tests rather than the client.

To the students struggling to learn this process I recommend that, after completing the histories and scoring all the tests, one take a few minutes to think about the client and to ask oneself what the best way would be of representing the client to other people. In the case of many clients it may be useful to thread together all the data using one of the following schemes:

(a) The developmental scheme, in which the author looks at the subject from the point of view of the influences that the person has had through the years and the way that he or she has reacted to the different stages in life.

(b) The personality scheme, which starts with a description of the basic personality style, and goes on to look at the life situation that the person is facing and the interplay between the personality style and the environmental forces.

(c) The differential diagnosis scheme, based on exploring the diagnostic issues that the patient presents and how the history and the test data can be used to clarify those issues.

Developmental Scheme: Report Example

Mr. Joseph Laggen is a 35-year-old white married man who was admitted to the hospital for the treatment of a depression. The patient associated his emotional problems with the fact that his wife has been very successful in establishing herself in her new career as a computer data analyst. The depression apparently included difficulty sleeping, a loss of energy and motivation, a loss of self-confidence, irritability, tension, and a tendency to cry. Mr. Laggen felt guilty about extramarital affairs that he has had in the past. He feared that his wife would become interested in other men and would leave him. Finally, he was easily upset by seemingly minor things, like the horoscope that told him that "a part of [his] life was coming to an end." On admission, his affect was seen as constricted and the mood was depressed.

Psychiatric History

Mr. Laggen claimed that he has "been depressed all of [his] life." He first received treatment, however, in 1979, when he was seen by Dr. Richard Stockton in Orlando, Florida. Although he was experiencing dizzy spells at the time, that complaint was seen as part of his depression. A year later, Mr. Laggen went to the Dickens Medical Center requesting an evaluation for the dizziness. He was seen by a neurologist there, but the evaluation revealed no abnormalities. After a referral to Psychiatry, he was seen as an outpatient at that facility for three months.

In 1984 Mr. Laggen saw Dr. Robert Clark on two occasions. He was subsequently hospitalized at the Webster Community Hospital under the care of Dr. Frederick Sedgwick, where he received medications as part of his treatment. The patient discontinued the medication after his discharge but then went to Tolan Community Hospital, where he received six electroshock treatments as an outpatient. He remembers improving as a result of this treatment. Finally, several weeks prior to the present hospitalization, Mr. Laggen received a prescription for amitriptyline from Dr. Sedgwick, but he stopped taking the medication after a week or so because of the side effects that he was experiencing.

Medical History

Mr. Laggen suffers from arthritis in both his shoulders and his hands. He uses ibuprofen in order to relieve the pain. The patient had an episode of bronchial asthma some time ago but, otherwise, the medical history is completely normal. A computed tomographic scan of the brain taken recently was reportedly within normal limits.

Family History

Mr. Laggen was born and raised in the Miami area, the third of seven siblings. Both of his parents are now deceased. The father was a plumber, an "outgoing" man who was frequently involved in different community organizations. Although he supported the patient in many projects and was fond of praising him for his persistence, he would depreciate him by saying that the patient "didn't know what he was doing" when he tried, for instance, to fix his car. A hard-working man, the father provided for the family well. The father liked to have "a shot and a beer" after work, but he never missed work because of his drinking and his intoxication never caused any problems at home.

The mother, on the other hand, was a "homebody" who did not like to go out of the house. She was shy and withdrawn and was probably uncomfortable with people. Mr. Laggen sees himself as being similar to his mother in this respect.

The patient has two older sisters who are Miami housewives and have never presented any major problems. The sister who follows him is also a housewife, but she has been depressed in the past. A brother comes next; he is divorced and has had trouble as a result of conflicts with his ex-wife. This brother works as a driver's helper on a beer delivery truck. There is another brother, who has his own business which deals with the covering of pool tables, and another sister, who is a housewife.

Mr. Laggen has been married for twelve years. His wife had been married before and has a son from her first marriage. Her first husband was a "rotten guy" who used to "beat her up" and even "brought other women home." The wife reportedly married the first husband because he had fathered her son and she felt that she should "give him a chance." The marriage took place after the birth of the baby and lasted only four months.

Mr. Laggen was apparently ambivalent about his marriage for years and had a series of extramarital affairs, some of which were known to the wife. He used to blame her for the financial difficulties of the family since she was inclined to "pester" him until he agreed to buy something she wanted, even when they could not afford it. For many years she worked outside of the home cleaning houses; this activity allowed her to make a reasonable additional income, but she felt "degraded" by the work. Recently she received training as a computer data analyst and changed her occupation. This has actually created some problems for the patient, since his own job no longer looks so clearly superior to hers. The wife has also managed to lose a significant amount of weight, so that he sees her as being more attractive. As a result, he is now fearful that his wife may have extramarital affairs or may become interested enough in another man that she would want to leave him. During the interview he talked about the chance that she would meet a man, now that she has a new profession, who would be more "intelligent" or emotionally "stable" than he. These fears have also generated some guilt about the fact that he "cheated" on her before.

Mr. Laggen has a 10-year-old adoptive son with whom he has a "real good relationship." Luke just graduated from junior high school, where he barely made it scholastically. However, he is well behaved and has never posed any other problems.

Eric (9) was born of the present marriage. He is a "hyper" individual who tends to "get down" when he does not obtain what he is after. Mr. Laggen fears that Eric may turn out to have emotional problems like himself. On the other hand, Eric has done very well in school: he is taking accelerated classes and is about three years ahead in reading ability.

Educational History

After attending St. Mark's Grammar School, the patient went on to graduate from St. Juniper High School in Miami. He remembers being a poor student who did just enough to "get by." At the instigation of his father, the patient attended a junior college, but he dropped out three weeks after classes started. In 1973 and 1974, however, Mr. Laggen was able to attend a welding school at Belden Tech and Parker Trade schools in Miami.

Occupational History

After completing his schooling, Mr. Laggen obtained a job at the electric company with the help of a brother-in-law. Rather than be drafted, he joined the Naval Reserve and was on active duty during 1971 and 1972. The patient spent much of this time aboard the USS Connecticut and remembers "hating it" at first but eventually adjusting well to military life.

When his active duty was completed, Mr. Laggen returned to the electric company. He was employed as a laborer at first, but after he completed his training as a welder, he transferred into a job that used his new skills. It appears that the patient enjoys his present position but feels that he should have done better. He talked about the fact that he reads business magazines and dreams of becoming a businessman himself. At other times, however, he tells himself that he does not have the ability it would take and that he would be a failure if he tried any other career.

Mental Status Examination

At the time of the evaluation the patient was alert, oriented, verbal, and coherent. Speech and language functions were intact. The other intellectual functions examined were also within normal limits. These included memory, calculations, figure reproductions, mental control, and abstractions. The thought process was always relevant, but the patient tended to be circumstantial and disorganized. The thought content was remarkable in the guilt over past extramarital affairs and the preoccupation with low self-esteem issues. The affective response was always appropriate. The mood demonstrated some range of emotions but was generally sad. The patient cried on several occasions while talking about his problems. Suicidal ideation was obviously present, but he did not have a plan at the time of the evaluation. No homicidal feelings were verbalized. The psychomotor activity and anxiety levels were within normal limits. Mr. Laggen was friendly and cooperative and posed no problems during the test administration.

Test Results

Millon Clinical Multiaxial Inventory (MCMI)
  Personality Structure Scales
  Introverted/schizoid, Base Rate Score = 99
  Inhibited/avoidant = 108
  Cooperative/dependent = 104
  Dramatic/histrionic = 21
  Confident/narcissistic = 10
  Competitive/antisocial = 12
  Disciplined/compulsive = 40
  Conflictual/passive-aggressive/explosive = 96
  Process Disorder Scales
  Schizotypal/schizoid = 92
  Borderline/cycloid = 82
  Paranoid/paraphrenic = 42
  Symptom Formation Scales
  Anxiety = 110
  Somatic preoccupations = 92
  Hypomania = 28
  Dysthymia = 103
  Alcohol abuse = 60
  Drug abuse = 8
  Psychotic thinking = 78
  Psychotic depression = 87
  Psychotic delusion = 55
  Validity = OK

Rorschach Inkblot Test
The results of this test will be incorporated into the section below.

The Thematic Apperception Test (TAT)
The results of this test will be incorporated into the section below.

Discussion

Mr. Laggen's childhood history suggests that the parents had an over-adequate-underadequate type of marital relationship. The father was an assertive and "outgoing" individual, a person who portrayed a secure image of competence. In contrast, the "shy and withdrawn" mother was "afraid of people" and was much less of a dominant figure. During those early years Mr. Laggen seems to have identified with the mother: he recalled that the father "would put [him] down" and remembered feeling very unsure of himself. The fact that he did not excel at anything may have been partly due to the introjected image of himself as an incapable individual. During the interview, for instance, there was evidence that several of his intellectual functions were somewhat above the average range. He, however, did not take advantage of this gift as a child, did poorly in school, and presently has an underdeveloped expressive language as a result. The fact that he did not excel in turn reinforced the low self-esteem.

The similarities between Mr. Laggen now and his mother as he described her are striking. According to the MCMI, the central traits in his personality are a fear of rejection, feelings of inadequacy, and a tendency toward mood changes. The scores suggest that Mr. Laggen wants very much to be liked by others but feels that it is much too likely that his social approaches will be rejected.

Mr. Laggen is probably a dependent and cooperative individual. Persons with similar MCMI personality profiles usually underestimate themselves: when they compare themselves to others, they feel that they are less capable, less attractive, or worth less as human beings. They tend to be unassertive people who seldom demand anything from others, although they can be controlling in a dependent and submissive manner. Similar individuals seem more comfortable when they can rely on others to make the important decisions and to offer them guidance and protection. The feelings of inadequacy are consistent with the fear of rejection, since similar individuals assume that people will eventually develop uncomplementary opinions about them and would not want to relate to them. As a result of his basic personality structure, Mr. Laggen tends to be apprehensive when relating to others. Probably seen as a shy and nervous individual, he is likely to feel uncomfortable in social situations. This type of person is often caught in a bind: on one hand, he would like very much to interact with others and to be liked and appreciated. On the other hand, he tends to avoid social situations in order to avoid the anxiety that these situations evoke.

The psychic conflict may be seen behaviorally in a vacillation or ambivalence that Mr. Laggen may have. At times he may be more open and friendly; at other times he will seem aloof, distant, abrasive, moody, or disinterested in others. Occasionally similar individuals may project the feelings created by the frustration of their basic conflict. In such instances, they may be more distrusting, or become hostile and prone to blame others for their failures. This pattern, however, will be short-lived, and eventually these individuals come back to feeling inadequate and blaming themselves for anything bad that happens to them.

The ambivalence and indecisiveness that the characterological conflicts lead into can be seen in some of the TAT stories. On card 1, for instance, the boy gets his violin after "bugging" his parents "for a long time" and then does not know if he wants to play it. That story was followed by the following anecdote, given to card 2:

> This reminds me of this young girl that wants to leave the farm because ... this isn't the life that she really wants. She doesn't want to work the land the rest of her life so she appears to be going off to school to study, to learn other areas and she looks like she feels pretty bad about doing what she has to do or what she feels she has to do, but she is going to do it anyway. ... She feels like she is deserting her mother and father even though it's not the life that she wants to choose. ... I think she will end up coming back.

In both cases the protagonist appeared so conflicted over what direction to take that the goal could not be pursued in an unequivocal and rewarding manner.

Like the girl in his story, Mr. Laggen was encumbered by his own feelings of inadequacy and his infantile attachment to the family of origin when he reached the period of early adulthood. In spite of the high aspirations, which were not unlike those of the child wanting the violin, he seemed more comfortable in a noncompetitive situation, in jobs felt to be below his level of ability, and with a wife who was too overweight to be desirable. To his credit, the patient had developed enough psychologically to be able to establish himself, both socially and occupationally, apart from his parents. Thus, in spite of his feelings of inadequacy, he has been able to make a reasonable adjustment most of the time and only occasionally becomes symptomatic.

Mr. Laggen's chronic ambivalence seems to have played a role in the developments that led up to the present crisis. Plagued by financial problems, he had encouraged his wife to work outside of the home and had later supported her becoming a computer data analyst. It seemed that he had not quite visualized what the future was bringing and, when the changes actually took place, like the protagonists in his TAT stories, he was no longer sure that he wanted what he had.

Two other elements also contributed to his discomfort with his wife's new life. First, there is the issue of the patient's own perception that he is an underachiever. Mr. Laggen feels that he should have done better occupationally even though his low self-esteem and his ambivalence have prevented him from trying another career. His wife's recent success as a computer analyst seems to have generated a midlife evaluation of his career status and goals, even though he apparently enjoys his trade very much.

Part of the issue in the career reevaluation is that of perceived status in the home. Although the patient often feels inadequate and has a low self-esteem, the lesson he learned in his childhood home was that the man is the master of the house. The new developments in his wife's life threatened the balance that had been established in the marriage from his point of view. Notice, for instance, the wish-fulfilling fantasy obtained on the blank card of the TAT:

> I think of a scene about me holding my wife and this time me being the stronger of the two, me being her "knight in shining armor," me being able to comfort her in any kind of problems. . . . Tell her that . . . I'm strong enough to protect her from anything, that's what I want to see me as, a strong individual, a more intelligent individual, a stronger individual. . . .

The story obviously betrayed a need to feel superior to his wife. Not having that position seemed threatening enough to elicit homicidal ideas, as suggested by the following story:

> This guy just looks like he murdered his wife and he's crying about it now. He felt he had to do it, but in a moment of craze, and now he's crying about it. . . . She must have drove him to it some way, I don't know, maybe she was cheating on him. . . . [card 13MF]

The psychological pain that Mr. Laggen has experienced as a result of his current crisis has been accompanied by a high level of anxiety and a significant depression, judging from the test results. Suicidal ideation was also apparently present. On the other hand, there were no signs of problems in his contact with reality nor were there any intellectual impairments. The fact that he has been able to establish stable relationships and has done acceptably well occupationally speak to the expectation that he will be able to work through his present problems and reinstate a balance in his life.

Diagnostic Formulation

I—Depressive episode
    Marital problem
II—Dependent personality disorder
III—No known medical problems contributing

Recommendations

Mr. Laggen would benefit from individual and family therapy designed to explore some of the issues discussed above. It would be most helpful if he could use these resources in order to become more comfortable with who he is and what he has achieved by this stage in his life. Any changes that he wants to put into effect should represent a real attempt to fulfill his life rather than a neurotic reaction to the fact that his wife has been able to better herself.

Personality Scheme: Report Example

Mr. Adranik Pash is a 41-year-old Iranian man who went to see Dr. Smith at his wife's urging. It seemed that Mr. Pash had "pinched" or "slapped" his wife after she did something to "aggravate" him. While giving examples of such instances, he expressed his view that his wife had intentionally provoked him in each instance. He explained that there were cultural differences: in the Islamic culture in which both he and his wife were raised, women are expected to be "subservient" to their husbands and physical punishment of the wife is considered an acceptable practice. Mr. Pash felt that there was nothing emotionally wrong with him but he agreed to see Dr. Smith and to do the psychological testing because he himself wanted to know that there was nothing wrong. He obviously felt that if there was someone in the family who had emotional problems, it would be his wife rather than he.

Medical and Psychiatric History

Mr. Pash denied ever having significant medical problems or accidents. This is the first time that he has been seen by a mental health professional. A history of psychiatric disorders in the family was denied.

Family History

Mr. Pash was born in Turkey but went to Iran and was raised there from infancy. He came to the United States to go to college about 20 years ago. Mr. Pash's father died in 1985 at the age of 75. He was a very hard working man who did not believe in getting help from others and was able to overcome some financial hardships on his own. He was a "strict" man of high principles. The father was a businessman; he owned a tea plantation which was lost along the way but later on was in the textile business. Mr. Pash remembered how he was his father's favorite when he was small, a fact that undoubtedly offered some benefits but which also generated much jealousy and ill will on the part of his siblings. Mr. Pash explained that his wife feels that he is depressed as a result of his father's death. His own point of view, however, is that the father was already elderly and, even though he was not insensitive to the father's death, the loss did not represent an overwhelming problem for him.

Mr. Pash's mother is 70 years old and well. She is an "uneducated woman" who was, nevertheless, a good housewife and a "loving" mother.

Mr. Pash is the third in a family of six siblings. The older brother, Abdul (48), is married, has three children, and directs the family's textile business from Iran. The older sister, Azadeh (46), is married and has two children who are attending school in New York. The patient came next and is followed by Said (36). This brother is involved with the sale of the textiles that the family produces in Iran, and lives in New York. The patient does not get along with him nor with his brother Mashang (34). Mashang is in partnership with Said, is married and also lives in New York. The patient explained that these two brothers do not believe in the traditional hierarchy of the Islamic family and do not accept his authority over them as an older brother. This issue has led to enough conflicts among the three of them that Mr. Pash has avoided contact with them. The younger brother, Ruhollah (24), is single and works in the family business in Iran.

The patient still seems very attached to his family of origin, in spite of whatever disagreements there may have been. His investment seems to be much more with them than with his wife, to the extent that he consults them on how to handle his wife and has used them in order to check the veracity of statements made by his wife.

Mr. Pash married in 1978. This was the first marriage for both his wife and him. In the traditional way, the family had chosen several prospective brides, among whom were women of very reputable families and high potential. He had chosen his wife, who had done well in terms of completing medical school, in spite of the fact that she came from a socioethnic group that was considered inferior. The two of them did meet before the wedding and the wife promised to be "subservient" in the traditional Islamic manner. The patient feels that the wife has not kept her promise: she uses the familiar second person pronoun when addressing him rather than the more respectful and formal pronoun he would prefer and is constantly doing things to "aggravate" him. He spoke of incidents, for instance, when the wife would lie or fake some sort of emergency only to gain attention from him.

The wife is a neurologist. Mr. Pash recalled how his family generously supported both of them when he was going to school and she was in her residency. Furthermore, he feels that he has "sacrificed" his career for her in that, for instance, he moved to Denver when she obtained a fellowship position in that city. He feels that she is less appreciative of those sacrifices than she should be. On the other hand, Mr. Pash feels that his wife is not assertive enough in securing the status that she should have for her professional achievements: he feels that she is willing to accept a lesser salary than she should and has not made an effort to discard some of the old customs which may be seen in this country as uncivilized.

Mr. Pash has two children. Adranik Junior is 7 years old, and Trani is 6. Both of them are doing well and have presented no problems.

Educational History

Mr. Pash graduated from high school in Iran and then came to the United States. He studied at Clark State College in South Dakota but, after two years, decided to leave the school and come to Chicago to work. Eventually he attended the Chicago Teacher's College, where he obtained a Bachelor of Science degree.

Occupational History

Mr. Pash explained that he was a "househusband" while his wife was doing her residency and fellowship. He then started a textile business, in association with his family, which was conducted from his own home. In 1985, after deciding that he needed to have an office outside of the home, he went into business with a partner in Skokie, Illinois, operating out of the partner's basement. This business reportedly thrived, but last September the patient decided to end the partnership and go into business on his own. At the time of the present evaluation his older brother was in the city with the purpose of helping Mr. Pash establish an office that will serve to sell their textiles to retailers in this country.

Mental Status Examination

At the time of the evaluation the patient was alert, oriented, verbal, and coherent. Speech and language functions were intact. The patient had a slight accent but was able to communicate very easily. The other intellectual functions examined were also within normal limits. These included memory, calculations, figure reproductions, mental control, and abstractions. The thought process was orderly and effective. The thought content was remarkable only in his concern that he not be seen as having a significant psychiatric problem. The affective response was always appropriate. The mood was within normal limits and demonstrated a good range of emotions. There was no suicidal or homicidal ideation. The psychomotor activity and anxiety levels were within normal limits. The patient was friendly and cooperative and presented no problems throughout the evaluation.

Test Results

Millon Clinical Multiaxial Inventory (MCMI)
  Personality Structure Scales
  Introverted/schizoid, Basal Rate = 34
  Inhibited/avoidant = 29
  Cooperative/dependent = 85
  Dramatic/histrionic = 58
  Confident/narcissistic = 62
  Competitive/antisocial = 64
  Disciplined/compulsive = 73
  Sensitive/passive-aggressive = 19
  Process Disorder Scales
  Schizotypal/schizoid = 60
  Borderline/cycloid = 60
  Paranoid/paraphrenic = 61
  Symptom Formation Scales
  Anxiety = 80
  Somatic preoccupations = 75
  Hypomania = 5
  Dysthymia = 69
  Alcohol abuse = 40
  Drug abuse = 60
  Psychotic thinking = 58
  Psychotic depression = 39
  Psychotic delusion = 64
  Validity = OK

Rorschach Inkblot Test
  The results of this test will be incorporated into the section below.

The Thematic Apperception Test (TAT)
  The results of this test will be incorporated into the section below.

Discussion

  According to the MCMI findings, Mr. Pash tends to have a low self-esteem and an orderly and compulsive nature. Similar individuals hold the life assumption that other people are more capable, interesting, or valuable than they are. They are unconceited and personable and are often capable of forming strong interpersonal relationships with others. They aim to be as congenial as possible to those around them in order to secure the support they need. As a result, similar people tend to be fairly submissive or, at least, compliant. They shy away from competitive situations because such situations make them feel unsupported and vulnerable. When they feel protected, however, they tend to be quite at ease and free of conflict.

Thus, one way in which Mr. Pash defends against the insecurity that his low self-esteem may bring is by counting on the guidance and protection of others. The second defense mechanism that he uses is thinking that, if he manages to avoid "making a mistake," he can always expect the outcome to be a positive one. Individuals with similar "compulsive" bents are orderly and plan for the future. They prepare in a conscientious manner and do the work on schedule. They try to be efficient, dependable, industrious, and persistent. Often these individuals relate in an overly respectful and ingratiating manner. However, they may be somewhat perfectionistic and demanding. Similar individuals believe in discipline and practice self-restraint, keeping their own emotions well under control. They may tend to be indecisive before they have had a chance to study all possible alternatives and have secured the needed support. The compulsive inclination may also serve to strengthen the feelings of inadequacy that are beneath it in that, whenever bad events take place, Mr. Pash will be inclined to look for what mistakes he may have made that could have led to the undesirable outcome.

It is possible to understand the dilemmas that Mr. Pash is currently facing in terms of his basic personality style. The patient's cooperativeness or dependency, for instance, may have played a role in his not having high aspirations for himself. TAT cards designed to elicit achievement motivation invariably produced stories that betrayed his insecurities or lack of high goals. Notice, for instance, the story obtained on card 1:

> This looks like a boy who was very interested in music. Finally he got the instrument and now he is thinking [about] how to use it. He looks pretty confused at present but he definitely seems to have an interest in it and will be able to play the violin. Maybe not as a musician, but he will be able to play that instrument.

The story appeared to take for granted the young fellow's inadequacy and seemed to argue for the approach of making the best out of marginal talents. Similarly, a TAT picture that is often associated with an eloquent circus performance yielded the story of a man escaping from prison instead. It is possible that the origin of both the cooperative trait and the modest aspirations in life can be found in the relationship that Mr. Pash had with his father. The favorite son, he may not have had to do much to earn a role in the family other than remaining cooperative, admiring, and receptive.

Also consistent with the personality make-up is Mr. Pash's continued dependence, emotional and financial, on his family of origin. It is ironic that the first person who fostered this dependency may have been his father, who was remembered admiringly as a person who pulled himself up by his bootstraps and would not consider asking other members of the family for help when he was in financial straits. Although the patient's financial dependency on his own family is made more feasible by the Islamic culture's sense for the extended family unit, the father's example served to illustrate that the way the patient has handled his financial responsibilities is significant even in his own culture. Obviously, even those cultures that emphasize the sharing of the extended family assets evaluate higher those family members who add to the family wealth.

Mr. Pash may have married well in terms of his particular personality style. His capable wife could become the kind of "rock of Gibraltar" who can comfortably support the emotional needs of a cooperative personality style. Several TAT stories, for example, have a "calm, quiet, and serene" woman successfully tranquilizing the male protagonist, or "changing his mind," or giving him useful advice. Thus, the question of why currently there are problems in the relationship is important enough to warrant some speculation.

The patient has both traditional Islamic values and a disciplined streak in his personality make-up. Both of these would lead him to emphasize a hierarchical view of the family. The changing times, with women becoming increasingly insistent on a position of parity; the immigration to the United States, where the "subservient" woman the patient may see as ideal would be seen as suffering from a character disorder; and the wife's occupational superiority have all conspired to make Mr. Pash's wife much less respectful and submissive than he would like. The physical "punishment" that Mr. Pash has used may be seen as an ill-fated attempt on his part to reestablish the supremacy that he no longer enjoys.

Often in similar cases the pain of adjustment is not one-sided: the other spouse also experiences difficulties, albeit of a different nature, in making the necessary changes. If there is any truth to the patient's claim that his wife does not conduct herself in a way that is in keeping with her status in our society, or that she has a way of finding what would really mortify him and using that information to "aggravate" him, these may be signs of her own ambivalence in shedding the traditional Islamic woman's role.

Turning back to interpretations that are closer to the test data and less speculative, the other finding that seemed worth noting is the fact that Mr. Pash gave an inordinate number of mythical or "evil" associations to inkblots at the expense of human responses. Possible cultural differences aside, in an American this finding would be interpreted as implying a tendency to distant other people in interpersonal relationships and to experience discomfort when an emotional relationship becomes too involved.

The mental status examination indicated that Mr. Pash does not have any cognitive or memory deficits. The impression was that he is a person of at least average intellectual abilities. The patient is a likeable individual who seemed reasonably open and well-meaning. The contact with reality reflected in his Rorschach responses was good, and there were no major signs of significant psychopathology. In other words, even though the life issues that he is struggling with most probably reflect his own personality structure, the issues are easily understood as part of human relationships.

Diagnostic Assignments

   I—Adjustment disorder with disturbance of conduct
      Marital problem
  II—Dependent and compulsive personality traits with no personality disorder
 III—No known medical problems contributing

Recommendations

Mr. Pash may benefit from a limited period of psychotherapy designed to help him explore the issues that he is facing in the changing relationship between himself and his wife. Family therapy may also be considered as a way of engaging the wife in a process that inevitably will involve both of them.

Diagnostic Scheme: Report Example

Susan McCormick is a 24-year-old single white woman who was admitted into the psychiatric unit at her own request when she felt that she was no longer able to function. She complained of mood fluctuations, explaining that there had been periods of depression occurring intermittently with periods of hypomanic behavior. The mood changes have been occurring more frequently so that the moods, instead of lasting a few months, recently have been changing almost daily. She characterized the days that preceded her admission as a mixture of both depression and hypomania: she did not sleep for three days, had suicidal thoughts, varied in her appetite, was spending too much money, could not think clearly, had racing thoughts, and felt nervous. Susan also talked about hearing the stereo even though the equipment was off.

The present evaluation was requested in order to clarify the diagnostic picture. Susan was admitted with the diagnosis of an acute manic episode, but the possibility of a bipolar affective disorder, a cyclothymic personality disorder, and/or alcohol abuse were being considered. At the time of the testing, the patient was taking lithium carbonate (300 mg q.i.d.). The course of treatment during hospitalization had been unremarkable.

Psychiatric History

This is the second psychiatric admission for this patient. The first admission took place at Baker's Hospital under the care of Dr. Robert Smith in August of 1982. At the time the patient was reportedly experiencing mood swings but was also thought to present psychotic features. She was treated with thiothixene (Navane), a medication that the patient continued to take for three months following her discharge from the hospital.

Susan recalled that during the summer of 1985 she was elated and "high," while in the fall of the same year she reported being "depressed." However, she did not receive any treatment until the present admission in the hospital.

Susan characterized her behavior when she is "high" as including feelings of elation, shopping sprees, and at least one sexual affair that she considered as showing poor judgment. The patient also admitted to drinking as much as eight beers a day on an intermittent basis.

The family history is remarkable in that the mother has reportedly suffered from depression throughout her life. The patient also has one brother who was hospitalized in a psychiatric ward as a result of his "violent episodes." Finally, apparently many, if not all, of her six brothers were said to be inclined to abuse alcohol.

Medical History

Susan had an ulcer in 1976. In 1982, while the patient was in the psychiatric ward, abnormalities on her EEG were found even though the results of a CT scan of the brain were within normal limits. The patient was then seen by Dr. David McMahon at Baker's Hospital, who put her on a regimen of anticonvulsant medication. This medication was discontinued in 1984. Upon seeing the patient during the present hospitalization, Dr. McMahon recommended keeping her off the medication unless an EEG showed abnormalities at this time.

In 1984 Susan was involved in a major car accident and suffered internal injuries, broken ribs, a bruised kidney and lung, and a hairline fracture of the spinal column. A laparotomy and splenectomy were done at South Town Community Hospital, where she was taken after the accident.

Abnormal lab findings on admission suggested the presence of a thyroid dysfunction; the patient was seen on consultation by Dr. Fernando Garcia, and a work-up was in progress at the time of the testing. Dr. James Wehner was consulted about hypertrophic scarring of the surgical incisions made at the time of the car accident, but he recommended no treatment at this time. Finally, Susan complained of having a discharge from her breasts during the last year.

Family History

Susan was born and raised in the Omaha area. Her father, a man in his seventies, was diagnosed as having a cancer of the prostate gland last May and is currently being treated with radiation. Despite his past tendency to always be "happy" and "look at things on the bright side," lately he has been talking about dying, an issue that upset several members of the family the last time they were together. The father is an "intelligent" man who "dresses well" but is "sharp with his tongue." He worked as an electrician at the Sanitary District, was eventually involved with the union as well, and has been retired for the last six years.

The mother is also in her seventies and has been depressed about the father's illness of late. At this time she does not seem able to forget bad things that have happened in the past, such as the death of a son who contracted multiple sclerosis and the fact that her sister had to be placed in a nursing home. The mother was always a "good mother" but was inclined to lead a constricted life because she was "afraid of a lot of things." For instance, the mother never learned how to drive a car. Mrs. McCormick is a social person who has "a lot of friends."

Susan is the youngest of eight siblings. Mark (45) is the oldest; he is an electrician who lives in California, is married, and has five children. The second oldest was Jonathan, who died in 1983 of multiple sclerosis when he was 40 years old. He was survived by a wife and four children. Although Rudy (42) was supposed to be the "slowest one," he has done better than anyone else, according to the patient. He is married, has three children, and works as an electrician. Bart (39) was described as being very immature, a "big baby" who in spite of being married and having five children lives only a few blocks away from the parents and is still very much connected with them. Bart has had three psychiatric hospitalizations and was described as a "nervous" person. John (36) is a salesman who lives in Florida. John has a college education and completed some work toward a master's degree. Although he is an "intelligent" person who is "very well read," John "drinks too much," tends to be arrogant, and has been divorced and remarried. The next brother also obtained a college education and is now employed as a data processor. Mike (34) is married. He has one child, and his wife is pregnant with a second. Susan feels emotionally closer to Michael than to anyone else in the family. The brother immediately preceding the patient is Peter (32). He is a musician but has not been able to earn a living playing the drums and works at a variety store in order to support himself. He moved out of the home at the age of 19 and eventually married. When this relationship ended in divorce recently, Peter moved back into the home of his parents. As a result, he shares with the patient the distinction of still living at home.

As she talked about her brothers, the patient seemed very competitive and inclined to criticize them. In fact, at one point she stated, "I guess I have a lot of hostility." The patient also complained about a cousin who is fifteen years her senior and who was partly raised by her parents since the cousin's father had died and her mother had to work. She admitted that the cousin had been very nice to her and was "always buying me things," but she seemed to resent the mothering that apparently came with the cousin's affection.

An important event in Susan's life was the car accident in June of 1984, in which her boyfriend was killed. The patient had been going out with this man for three years when the accident occurred. They had started going together when she was 19 years old and he was 27, a difference in age which partly reflected the character of the relationship. Susan talked about the fact that she was always accepting his opinion and changing her own behavior to comply with his wishes. She now feels that she was denying her own self and that her submissiveness came out of her insecurity. The accident took place when the boyfriend, who often drove too fast, unexpectedly lost control of the car and drove it into a tree. Susan still has occasional nightmares about the accident.

Susan remembers herself as a "shy" and "nervous" person during her younger years. She talked about "daydreaming a lot," to the point that her involvement in her own fantasies worked to the detriment of the quality of her life. This problem has been mostly outgrown by now.

Susan talked about herself as a sociable individual with many friends. She has had several boyfriends in the last two years although she does not have a boyfriend at this time. The patient talked about two occasions on which she impulsively severed a romantic relationship in order to pursue the attentions of a nicer-looking man even though the latter was a "jerk." She went on to explain how she should have been able to appreciate the assets of a person who is not particularly good-looking. It was obvious that the patient was struggling with some of the normal issues of heterosexual relationships at this stage in her life.

Educational History

After attending the Walsh and the St. Gerard's grammar schools in Omaha, Susan went on to graduate from Gables High School. She tended to be an average student and had no significant problems academically.

Occupational History

After her high school graduation in 1980 the patient worked for three years as a switchboard operator. Since 1983, however, she has been a secretary at Bell & Howell. She likes her job and feels that she has been doing well in the company.

Mental Status Examination

At the time of the evaluation the patient was alert, oriented, verbal, and coherent. Speech and language functions were intact. The other intellectual functions examined were also within normal limits. These included memory, calculations, figure reproductions, mental control, and abstractions. The thought process was orderly and effective. The thought content was remarkable in the presence of neurotic preoccupations, such as her feelings of insecurity. Some preoccupation with the car accident was seen. The affective response was always appropriate. The mood was within normal limits much of the time, but the patient tended to talk about sad events in her life (the death of her boyfriend, her fights with her brothers, resentments that she has against her parents, and so on) and cried several times during the interview. There was no suicidal or homicidal ideation. The psychomotor activity and anxiety levels were within normal limits. Ms. McCormick was friendly and cooperative and presented no problems during the test administration.

Test Results

Millon Clinical Multiaxial Inventory (MCMI)
  Personality Structure Scales
  Introverted/schizoid, Basal Rate = 45
  Inhibited/avoidant = 75
  Cooperative/dependent = 96
  Dramatic/histrionic = 93
  Confident/narcissistic = 76
  Competitive/antisocial = 72
  Disciplined/compulsive = 5
  Sensitive/passive-aggressive = 104
  Process Disorder Scales
  Schizotypal/schizoid = 51
  Borderline/cycloid = 88
  Paranoid/paraphrenic = 67
  Symptom Formation Scales
  Anxiety = 105
  Somatic Preoccupations = 98
  Hypomania = 111
  Dysthymia = 88
  Alcohol Abuse = 99
  Drug Abuse = 91
  Psychotic Thinking = 62
  Psychotic Depression = 69
  Psychotic Delusion = 57
  Validity = OK

Rorschach Inkblot Test
The results of this test will be incorporated into the section below.

The Thematic Apperception Test (TAT)
The results of this test will be incorporated into the section below.

Discussion

The mental status examination gave no indications of intellectual deficits. The patient appeared to be of average intellectual abilities.

The issue of whether Ms. McCormick suffers from a bipolar affective disorder, however, could not be resolved as definitively. It seems that it will be necessary to wait some time so that one can have a more longitudinal view of her problems. The picture that emerged from looking at her psychological make-up at this particular time was unfortunately too ambiguous. On the Rorschach, for instance, the patient seemed impulsive and superficial, qualities that could be part of a manic episode. However, the protocol did not have any of the other markers that typify manic individuals. For instance, the number of responses was fairly low, and the associations did not have the excessive use of color and movement that often characterizes manic protocols. These findings were in keeping with the observations made during the testing: there was no pressured speech, inability to sit still, or any other manic symptom.

The MCMI, on the other hand, had an extremely high elevation on the Hypomanic Scale, which has been shown to be a good bipolar indicator. The pressure toward achievement that was occasionally seen in the TAT stories can also be cited in support of the bipolar diagnosis. There were indications of depression as well in that scores on both the Cycloid and Dysthymic scales of the MCMI were elevated. These elevations were consistent with the sadness and low self-esteem that often characterized the TAT protagonists. Finally, the histrionic element that came out as a predominant aspect of the personality style is commonly seen with individuals who have a bipolar affective disorder.

The MCMI scores showed that Ms. McCormick has a combination of dependent, histrionic, and hostile elements. This pattern suggested that Ms. McCormick is caught in the bind of having low self-esteem but feeling that she has to conceal her true self-appraisal of her worth and appear confident and self-assured. Individuals with similar scores tend to feel less gifted or valuable as human beings when they compare themselves to others. The low self-image usually leads to feelings of insecurity and anxiety when the individual is in a competitive situation. Similar people are followers rather than leaders, usually making an effort to be cooperative and to get along well with others. Part of this effort is to control and hide their own emotions, especially when they are feeling anger toward another person. Since her approach is one of trusting others to protect her and guide her, Ms. McCormick at times may not be well prepared to take responsibility for the attainment of life goals. In Ms. McCormick's case, the dependency seemed uncomfortable to her; she spent a great amount of time putting herself down for being so submissive during the interview and in the TAT stories.

The elevation in the histrionic scale of the MCMI indicated that Ms. McCormick also needs a certain amount of attention from others. Ms. McCormick may seek to be conspicuous and to have frequent affirmation of approval and affection. Individuals with similar profiles take an active role in involving others. They often develop a sensitivity to the feelings of the people around them and use this knowledge to evoke the reactions that they desire. They can be charming and outgoing, colorful, dramatic, or seductive.

Ms. McCormick may be friendly and cooperative at times when she is feeling more inadequate. Soon, however, she begins to feel that she should be projecting a different image and changes to a more arrogant and controlling posture. She may become bored with stable relationships and displace some of her inner conflicts into interpersonal resentments. Thus, she may seem moody and easily irritated, unpredictable, or negativistic.

It was the examiner's impression that the personality style was functional enough and did not constitute a personality disorder. Ms. McCormick came out slightly below the normal range in reality boundedness on the Rorschach. The fact that the scores were very close to the expected range and that Ms. McCormick appeared very intact clinically predicated against overestimating the problems that were found. Ms. McCormick appeared to be still suffering from a mild post-traumatic stress disorder. She has been bothered by nightmares about the accident, and expressed some guilt about not having shared with the boyfriend her ideas about the relationship before he died. In addition, she spent a sizable amount of time talking about the accident during the interview and told two TAT stories that were obviously related to the accident.

Psychological strengths could be found in the patient's intellectual intactness and the lack of a crippling emotional disturbance. Furthermore, Ms. McCormick seemed personable and has had some social and occupational successes in spite of the problems that she presented.

Diagnostic Impressions

I—Rule out bipolar affective disorder
   Rule out cyclothymic disorder
   Post-traumatic stress disorder
II—Dependent, histrionic, and passive-aggressive traits with no personality
   disorder
III—No known medical problems contributing

Recommendations

A period of continued evaluation will be necessary before diagnostic confidence can be attained. In the meantime, the use of psychotropic medications in order to control the symptomatology may be considered.

It would be beneficial if Ms. McCormick would commit herself to a psychotherapeutic involvement for a period of time. Besides the diagnostic value that the sessions may have, the patient may be able to use this resource to work through her feelings of inadequacy as well as the discomfort that she still experiences with regard to her accident.

IV.E. VOCATIONAL TESTING

In order to counsel an individual on occupational choices, the following factors have to be considered:
- (a) Abilities
- (b) Achievement motivation
- (c) Personality style
- (d) Field of interest
- (e) Income and employability requirements

The level of intellectual ability can be evaluated through an IQ test. When specific areas are being considered, more specialized tests (for instance, a test of manual dexterity or tests of mechanical abilities) can be used to determine the individual's capacity. The emotional ability to go through training is usually evaluated on the basis of history and present level of pathology. The client is usually interviewed for this material, although personality tests can also be used.

The client's motivation is also assessed clinically, by taking into account the client's comments about training as well as past efforts.

The client's personality style can be evaluated through a personality trait inventory (see recommendation under emotional evaluation).

Table 12 gives the relevant information concerning the vocational inventories that are commonly used.

The client's expectations regarding income and availability of work also have to be taken into consideration and discussed.

Recommended Report Outline

1. Reason for referral: the reason it is felt that the person needs a vocational evaluation.

TABLE 12. Commonly Used Vocational Inventories

Name	Scoring	Description
Career Assessment Inventory (CAI)	Auto	305-item questionnaire measuring three types of scales: (a) Occupational Theme Scales (6) describing the individual's overall work orientation (b) Basic Interest Scales (22) providing a measure of specific interests (c) Occupational Scales (89) relating individual's interests to those of persons in the different careers
Kuder Preference Record	Manual	498 items that rate the individual's preferences in 9 occupational areas: mechanical, computational, scientific, persuasive, artistic, literary, musical, social service, and clerical
Strong-Campbell Interest Inventory (SCII)	Auto	325-item revision of the Strong Vocational Interest Blank. Recommended for individuals interested in careers that require advance training. The test measures three types of scales as described above: (a) General Occupational Theme Scales (6) (b) Basic Interest Scales (23) (c) Occupational Scales (24)

2. Educational history
   (a) Amount of education completed
   (b) Degree of past academic success
   (c) Attitudes of the patient toward further education or training

3. Occupational history: jobs that the client has held in the past, together with the period of time the client held each job and the objective and subjective success attained.

4. Behavioral observations
   (a) Appearance
   (b) Quality of the examiner-client interactions
   (c) General behaviors (personal comments made, unusual behaviors, etc.)
   (d) Specific test behaviors (motivation, defensiveness, attitude)

5. Test results: whenever possible, list the actual scores.

6. Discussion
   (a) General level of abilities
   (b) Abilities that differ from this general level (weaknesses and strengths)
   (c) Personality style
   (d) Fields of interest
   (e) Amount of motivation
   (f) Occupations that fit enough of the issues addressed above to be good alternatives for this patient

7. Recommendations: what the patient should do, in the light of all the information given, in order to improve vocational adjustment or opportunity.

Report Example

Mr. G. is a 46-year-old white man who seems capable but has been unemployed for the past nine years. The patient carries a diagnosis of undifferentiated schizophrenia. At this time, he expresses a wish to receive vocational rehabilitation.

Educational History

Mr. G. was raised in the Chicago area, where he went to a Catholic elementary school until he finished the primary grades. He recalls having no difficulties and always passing to the next grade at the end of the year. However, he was not a very good student, nor was he motivated toward academic achievement. The patient continued his education by attending a public high school. He was then most interested in the science courses, although he tended to get poor grades. Mr. G. failed some courses and had some trouble studying the material during the high school years, but he nevertheless managed to graduate. Since that time he has not involved himself in any kind of training or education.

Occupational History

After his high school graduation, Mr. G. did not have a clear idea of what he wanted to do with his life. He did want to leave his family of origin and felt that enlisting in the military service would be a practical way of accomplishing this end. During the four years that followed, the patient served in the Army, stationed at different locations of the United States. He did not particularly like some of the limitations that the military forced on him but was fairly well adjusted and productive during this time. Upon discharge, he was able to obtain a job as a bank teller, which he held for ten years. At first, he was able to perform his duties well and was reasonably happy with his job. During the last few years, however, he had become very discontented, did not feel supported and appreciated by his superiors, and his emotional problems became increasingly more intrusive. Nine years ago he was given a sick leave while he was in the hospital and, when he ran out of sick leave, his employment was terminated. At the time Mr. G. felt relieved by the firing, and he has never attempted to get back into a regular job in any serious manner since then.

Behavioral Observations

Mr. G. was very interested in being examined and was cooperative throughout the four test sessions. With each succeeding examination period, Mr. G. became less anxious, showing greater temerity and less hesitancy, uttered more direct statements and fewer questions, and was able to hold more casual and unguarded conversations with the examiner.

Initially, the patient sought out the examiner to protest the difficulty of the Strong Vocational Inventory and required encouragement to continue. During the WAIS administration, Mr. G. was intermittently anxious, shaking his legs, rapidly smoking cigarettes, and clicking his tongue against his teeth. Yet when he engaged in a personally meaningful task, like the Arithmetic subtest, his anxious behavior markedly subsided or stopped.

Test Results

Wechsler Adult Intelligence Scale
  Full Scale IQ = 92
  Verbal Scale IQ = 95
  Performance Scale IQ = 89
  Information, scaled score = 8
  Digit Symbol = 8
  Comprehension = 9
  Picture Completion = 9
  Arithmetic = 12
  Block Design = 6
  Similarities = 10
  Picture Arrangement = 9
  Digit Span = 6
  Object Assembly = 6
  Vocabulary = 9

Millon Clinical Multiaxial Inventory (MCMI)
  Personality Structure Scales
  Introverted/schizoid, Basal Rate score = 32
  Inhibited/avoidant = 82
  Cooperative/dependent = 81
  Dramatic/histrionic = 30
  Confident/narcissistic = 9
  Competitive/antisocial = 24

Disciplined/compulsive = 112
Sensitive/passive-aggressive = 80
Process Disorder Scales
Schizotypal/schizoid = 75
Borderline/cycloid = 65
Paranoid/paraphrenic = 40
Symptom Formation Scales
Anxiety = 86
Somatic preoccupations = 65
Hypomania = 77
Dysthymia = 74
Alcohol abuse = 29
Drug abuse = 49
Psychotic thinking = 69
Psychotic depression = 63
Psychotic delusion = 56
Validity = OK

Intellectual Assessment

The WAIS Full Scale score indicated that Mr. G. is functioning at the lower end of the normal range of intelligence. Despite the presence of some test anxiety, this score was thought to be representative of his current capability.

Emotional Assessment

Mr. G.'s obsessive-compulsive nature permeates all of the testing results. Its effect can also be seen in the three main areas of emotional functioning: the cognitive area, the inner emotional (intrapersonal) area, and the interpersonal area.

From a cognitive point of view, Mr. G.'s perceptions tend to center on the small aspects of reality. This is shown in the Rorschach results by overuse of the small and unusual details. The patient's perceptions also tend to be rigid and concrete. Again, in the Rorschach, there is a tendency to base most responses on the form of the blot only, without taking into account the more intangible aspects of the stimuli. His obsessive tendency is particularly obvious in the WAIS, where his highest score was on Arithmetic, a subtest where orderliness and meticulousness pay off.

In their personal habits, obsessive-compulsive individuals tend to be efficient, dependable, industrious, and persistent. Often they believe in discipline and practice self-restraint in a perfectionistic fashion.

The compulsive behavior style colors the way that Mr. G. relates to others. The number of human responses that he gave on the Rorschach, for instance, was minimal, suggesting that the patient does not relate often to people. Since the obsessive-compulsive tendency is often seen as a maneuver to gain distance from others, the finding fits in well. The findings also make sense because people tend to be less reliable than nonhumans, and obsessive-compulsives look for situations that are structured in such a way that they can always predict the outcome. We can also speculate that, when he does relate to others, he will tend to relate in a submissive manner with those who have a higher status and in a dominant manner with those of lower status. Finally, it can also be speculated that he will have some definite expectancies with regard to the roles that others will play in relationships with him.

It should be noted that when we refer to Mr. G. as having an obsessive-compulsive personality style, the label is not used to indicate a type of pathology. The label is used merely to describe a flavor of his particular personality that involves the traits discussed. The use of this label does not mean to imply the presence of a neurosis or of a character disorder.

In any event, given this personality style, it is not hard to understand the type of situation that has gotten Mr. G. into trouble in the past. Problematic situations have been of two types: the first is the situation in which Mr. G. has a particular expectancy from others that is not fulfilled. For instance, on several occasions, Mr. G. has demanded a specific action from therapists. When his demands are not met, the patient becomes very disturbed. As discussed above, the obsessive-compulsive tends to have a well-conceptualized set of expectations. When others do not behave as expected, the basic premise of order and predictability is undermined, and the experience is perceived as upsetting.

The second problematic situation has been the scheduling and ordering of the patient's time in a meaningful manner. Mr. G. finds himself with a lot of free time due to his prolonged disability. The lack of a meaningful schedule and a productive life is especially troublesome for a person who has rigid obsessive and perfectionistic goals.

Often the patient's coping mechanisms break down when he is faced with one of the problem situations. His behavior is then marked by restlessness and agitation. His anxiety was seen behaviorally in the testing sessions through his constant leg movement. The lowest scores of the WAIS was Digit Span, a subtest that is very sensitive to anxiety and a subsequent inability to concentrate. The Rorschach findings show the anxiety, as well as some potential for acting out.

The presence of avoidant personality traits and a tendency to withdraw from his relationships with others is also notable. However, there were no signs of a thought process disturbance or psychotic symptomatology.

Vocational Assessment

The Strong Vocational Inventory showed that Mr. G. is high on the "Conventional Theme" (score = 60). Subjects who score high on this theme:

... prefer jobs where they know exactly what they are supposed to do, using both verbal and numerical skills. They prefer office work but do not like to be leaders. They want to know exactly what is expected of them and generally prefer jobs that involve doing the same task over and over. They describe themselves as well controlled, reliable and stable. People with the following occupations have high scores on this theme: bank clerks, statisticians, financial analysts, accountants, office managers and bookkeepers.

On the Special Interest Scale of the Strong, the patient scored highest on adventurous occupations. This finding is hard to interpret because it does not fit at all with the rest of the information about the patient.

On the Strong Occupational Scales, Mr. G. scored high on "printer, math or science teacher, senior CPA, pharmacist, or computer programmer."

The Kuder Preference Record showed high scores on the clerical computational scales.

On the positive side, the interests shown on the Strong and Kuder inventories go along very well with the evaluation of the patient's ability and personality. His intellectual capacity is sufficient to warrant some sort of clerical training. The patient's obsessive-compulsive personality style would be an asset in the type of job where orderliness, meticulousness, and dependability are important. A negative consideration, however, is that the patient has been unemployed for a fairly long period of time and, in spite of persistent psychotherapy, has not been able to control adequately the periods of agitation.

Recommendations

Rather than continuing the unsuccessful attempts at "insight" therapy, I would suggest a vocational rehabilitation plan. The plan of most benefit to the patient would be training that would enable him to function as a clerk of some sort. This represents a good fit with the patient's interests, goals, and intellectual abilities and should be tried first.

In the event that the patient's emotional instability makes him unable to receive the training necessary, I feel that the patient should be helped to obtain a job at a maintenance or janitorial level. Although this will be less to the patient's liking, it would still provide some structure and fulfillment for Mr. G.

Neither one of the above goals can be accomplished without an ongoing and involved supportive psychotherapy program. The patient needs to feel at all times that there is an understanding and protective therapist on whom he can depend.

V Patient Management

V.A. THE PROBLEM-ORIENTED APPROACH

After the basic information about a patient has been gathered, the therapist needs to organize it in a comprehensive manner. The problem-oriented approach first developed by Hayes-Roth, Longabaugh, and Ryback (1972) provides a very good system for the beginner, since it provides a way of organizing one's thinking and forces the practitioner to consider and document all the steps necessary for good patient care.

Problem-oriented patient management calls for the following sequence:

(a) Construction of a problem list.

(b) Determination of treatment goals.

(c) Development of a treatment plan.

(d) Determination of the expected length and course of treatment.

(e) Negotiation of the treatment plan with the client so that a treatment contract is established through which all participants agree on the plan of action.

(f) Fulfillment of the treatment contract.

The problem list should include all the concrete issues presented by the individual that may be considered "problems." Although it is impossible to present an exhaustive list, common problems in the psychological areas of functioning are presented in Table 13.

The goals of treatment would have to be specified. These goals refer to the outcome of the treatment rather than the process used to achieve that outcome. Generally the goals are to reduce at least some of the problems presented in the list. In other words, a suitable goal may be to reduce the patient's anxiety; having the patient be more cognizant of his or her feelings is usually seen as the means through which the treatment goals may be pursued.

V.B. DEVELOPING A TREATMENT PLAN

As discussed in Chapter II, emotional difficulties can be seen as the result of friction between the individual and the environment. A treatment plan consists of the interventions that are proposed as a way of reducing this friction.

Attempts to reduce friction may involve changes in any one of the following spheres:

(a) The environment

(b) The organic make-up of the patient

113

TABLE 13. Problems Commonly Seen in Psychiatric Patients

Somatic Functions

Psychomotor acceleration, overtalkativeness, decreased need for sleep
Psychomotor retardation, loss of energy
Loss of appetite
Overeating
Insomnia
Hypersomnia
Stomach or intestinal trouble, ulcer, headache, asthma, dizzy spells, or other somatic complaints
Medical illness or disability
Alcohol or drug intoxication

Intellectual Functions

Intellectual deficiency
Memory deficiency
Language deficiency
Inability to concentrate
Short attention span
Confusion, incoherence, disorientation
Lack of ability to perceive or express emotion
Inability to make decisions
Tangentiality, flight of ideas, circumstantiality, irrelevancy
Preoccupations, obsessions

Intrapsychic Functions

Inappropriate emotional response
Fluctuations of mood, irritability, explosiveness
Sadness, guilt, feelings of unworthiness, feelings of hopelessness
Suicidal feelings
Elation, overconfidence, feelings of omnipotence
Lack of confidence, feelings of inferiority
Bizarreness, awkwardness
Untidiness, bad personal hygiene
Impulsiveness
Irresponsible behavior
Excessive need for attention
Tactlessness
Fears, phobias, anxiety, tension, agitation, restlessness
Feelings of depersonalization, feelings of unreality, unusual illusions or feelings
Rigidity, coldness, aloofness
Emotional constriction

TABLE 13. *(continued)*

Intrapsychic Functions (continued)

Denial, inability to accept an aspect of reality
Delusions
Hallucinations

Social Functions

Lack of friends, loneliness, withdrawal
Shyness, discomfort in relating to others, fear of rejection
Overdependence, oversubmissiveness
Argumentativeness, obstructionism
Hostility
Homicidal feelings
Antisocial behavior, tendency to take advantage of others
Loss of meaningful other
Grandiosity, arrogance
Mistrust, suspiciousness, paranoid feelings
Tendency to dominate or overcontrol others

Family Functions

Irritation with behaviors of other family members
Argumentativeness
Struggle for control, conflictual family system
Deficient communication in the family
Lack of differentiation of family members, united front family system
Irresponsible behavior by family member
Rejection of family member, scapegoating
Interference by relatives
Lack of participation in family decisions, overadequate-underadequate family
    system
Inadequate parenting
Lack of stability of family relationships, lack of strength of family relationships
Launching difficulties, inability of grown children to move out

Sexual Functions

Discomfort over homosexual tendencies
Wish to be of opposite sex, discomfort with sex-appropriate roles
Sexual overinhibition
Inability to get sexually aroused
Sexual promiscuity
Impotence, frigidity, repulsion by sexual thoughts

(continued)

TABLE 13. *(continued)*

Sexual Functions (continued)

Complaint of pain during sex
Inability to find sexual partner
Rejection by sexual partner
Attraction toward tabooed partner or abnormal object
Lack of information about sex, lack of sexual sophistication
Sexual incompatibility
Moral or legal problem resulting from individual's sexual behavior

---

Occupational Functions

Confusion over vocational or occupational goals
Unemployment, lack of schooling
Dissatisfaction with job or school

    (c) The patient's cognition
    (d) The patient's affective response
    (e) The patient's skills

The kind of relationship that the client is offered during psychotherapy is part of the environment that the person is exposed to at the time of treatment. One of the first issues that a therapist has to face in formulating a treatment plan is whether to emphasize "supportive" therapy as opposed to one that involves psychological changes by the individual. Supportive interventions usually involve changes in the environment and are typically not thought to lead to lasting personal changes. Frequently the therapist has to balance these two directions, which are commonly opposed to one another, since environmental changes take away the need or opportunity for the individual to respond in a different manner to problematic life issues. A lack of balance in the treatment plan can be expected to result in a less than optimal outcome. If the emphasis is unduly placed on environmental changes at the expense of personal change, the individual's needs may be gratified and the person may be able to function better; however, he or she will not be able to cope in a different way when a similarly troublesome environmental situation arises again. On the other hand, a treatment plan that calls only for personal growth and is not sensitive to the current needs of the individual could lead to further tension and an increase in psychopathology. Moreover, in the latter case, the patient may become intolerably frustrated and drop out of treatment.

The balance between the two directions should remain fluid and changeable. It can be argued, for instance, that the emphasis at the beginning of therapy should be that of making the environment fit the individual better, since the person is likely to be in a substantial amount of distress at that time and the therapist needs to find a way of consolidating the therapeutic alliance. In contrast, in the middle and late phases of treatment, the client may be less distressed and symptomatic and the therapist may not need to worry as much about being emotionally aligned with the client. The patient's motivation also has to be considered. Some clients come to treatment because they dislike some aspect of themselves that they clearly want to change; others may want to rid themselves of a symptom without going through the pain of looking at negative aspects of themselves or changing their behavior. A good therapist is able to take all of these issues into account when formulating the treatment plan.

As noted, one way of changing the environment is by presenting the client with a supportive relationship in the psychotherapeutic setting. How this may be done will be discussed in Chapter VI. In addition, there are several ways in which changes in the environment may be attempted. These include:

    (a) Changing the environment entirely by moving the client to a different place of residence.

    (b) Working to increase the tolerance of the environment for the problem that the patient presents.

    (c) Working toward decreasing aspects of the environment that are considered to be causing or contributing to the problem, or increasing aspects of the environment that are considered therapeutic.

    (d) Having the environment give appropriate reinforcements and recognitions for the patient's behavior.

    (e) Using hypnotic suggestions as a means through which a member of the environment (the therapist) can influence the patient's behavior.

Interventions directed toward changing the organic make-up of the patient may have the following goals:

    (a) Evaluating and treating a physical disorder that is considered causative or contributory to the problem in question.

    (b) Giving the patient a medical treatment that changes his or her reactions to the environment. This medical treatment usually consists of either psychotropic medications (see Chapter VI) or electroconvulsive therapy.

Changes in the patient's cognitive system are effected on the premise that altering the patient's self-perception and view of the world will lead to changes in the affective and behavioral spheres. Furthermore, some cognitive changes may be good in their own right, even if they do not lead to any other change. The interventions that can be made in this area include:

    (a) Increasing the patient's own awareness of the problem.

    (b) Adding information that the patient needs or correcting some misinformation that the patient has.

(c) Discovering and understanding secondary benefits that the patient obtains.

(d) Increasing the conscious motivation that the client has to work on the problems by exploring the negative consequences that the problem has in the person's life.

(e) Determining if there are any specific situations in the patient's life that are prone to evoking or exacerbating the problem.

(f) Exploring the historical dynamics or childhood origins of the problem.

The affective response refers to the feelings that the patient has about himself or herself or the world. Any changes that are made in the individual or the environment may end up changing the affective response. However, attempts are sometimes made to alter the emotional responses directly. These attempts include:

(a) Externalizing emotion, with the goal of venting feelings that are over-controlled or establishing contact with feelings that have been repressed.

(b) Working through of emotional material, a process that changes feelings through continued exposure and assimilation of situations similar to the situation that originally evoked the feelings in question.

Therapeutic training to improve the patient's skills can be:

(a) Corrective training, which may involve giving the patient a skill that he or she did not have or changing the pattern of behavior that is evoked in the patient by a particular situation.

(b) Compensatory training, which involves developing skills to cope with the problem rather than to solve it.

Table 14 gives a summary of the curative factors discussed.

Given all the possible options, a therapist may decide to concentrate all efforts on one singular plan or to attempt to integrate several plans. Although it is possible to integrate many of the plans, however, some plans actually work in opposite directions. When choosing curative plans, the therapist must take three factors into consideration:

(a) The ability of the patient to change.

(b) The theoretical orientation and training of the therapist.

(c) The financial or practical considerations involved.

When considering the patient's ability to change, four factors should be taken into account:

(a) The patient's intellectual abilities (patients who are very dull or have an organic brain deficit tend to have little ability to change).

(b) The patient's motivation (low motivation is a bad prognostic indication for change).

(c) The level of pathology. As a rule, the more disturbed the patient is, the less able he or she will be to change. However, a lack of distress is also a bad prognostic indicator, because it is then thought that the patient is "not hurting enough." The level of pathology may change

TABLE 14. Possible Therapeutic Plans

 1. Change of environment
 2. Increase in tolerance of environment
 3. Environmental reinforcements
 4. Positive environmental changes
 5. Hypnotic suggestions
 6. Treatment of physical disease
 7. Psychotropic medication
 8. Increase in awareness
 9. Offer of information
10. Exploration of secondary benefits
11. Exploration of negative consequences of patient's behavior
12. Exploration of current dynamics
13. Exploration of historical dynamics
14. Externalization of emotion
15. Working through
16. Corrective training
17. Compensatory training
18. Ego-syntonic support
19. Problematic support

while the patient is under treatment. When this happens, the patient's ability to change has to be reevaluated.

(d) The amount of social and family support that the patient has.
The lower the estimate of the patient's ability to change, the more reliance that must be placed on environmental or organic changes. As the ability to change increases, the treatment plans can rely more on cognitive, affective, or behavioral changes.

Schools of therapy often tend to emphasize one therapeutic plan more than others. The system presented here can be used by students from different orientations. It allows integration of the different orientations, such as the cognitive-behavioral integrations proposed by Arnold Lazarus for his multimodal therapy (1976).

Finally, because different treatment plans demand different amounts of time and degrees of involvement from the therapist, the practical issues of available resources also must be taken into consideration.

V.C. THE TREATMENT CONTRACT

The treatment contract involves a process by which the patient and the therapist discuss the current problems of the patient and reach some sort of understanding regarding the goals and method of therapy.

The treatment contract has a particular chronological place in the management of a patient. It should be formulated after the basic information has been gathered and before therapeutic efforts are made. Although it usually stays fairly constant, it should be flexible enough so that significant new developments can lead to renegotiation of the contract.

Some therapists emphasize the importance of the contract by having a contract that:

(a) Is a written document kept by both patient and therapist (or treatment staff).

(b) States concretely and specifically what each individual is agreeing to do.

(c) Has stipulations of measurable changes that would be taken as indications that the problem is improved or solved.

Although most therapists today do not insist on such intricate contracts, no one denies the importance of reaching a clear understanding with the patient regarding acceptable plans and expectations. In order to expedite this understanding the therapist should:

(a) Set an atmosphere in the treatment sessions that will be conducive to this type of negotiation (discussed later).

(b) Bring up the topic again when further discussion is needed.

V.D.   THE THERAPEUTIC STANCE

Therapists may be defined as individuals who have been trained to use themselves so as to help patients solve emotional difficulties in their lives. If this definition is accepted, it would follow that some characteristics may be generally important for any therapist to have. For instance:

(a) Therapists should be flexible individuals who do not have to act in a particular way because of personal needs but who can behave in whatever way may be thought to help patients the most.

(b) Therapists should be "professionals." They should be able to present themselves as individuals who are well trained for their particular job (or who are supervised by someone who is) and who would not take a case in which they could not do an adequate job. They should not be unduly nervous or fearful and should have some assurance in their ability to deal with treatment situations.

(c) Therapists should have a certain degree of empathy. They should be able to understand how patients experience the world, to have some sympathy for their problems, and to be interested in helping patients solve those problems.

(d) Therapists should be "genuine." They should be aware and accepting of their own feelings. This does not mean that therapists have to be an "open book." They can, indeed, choose which feelings would be productive to share with patients and which would not be. What it does mean is that whatever part of the therapist the patient sees should be real and not phony or put on.

(e) Therapists should have positive regard for patients. They should be able to accept patients at whatever level of functioning they are, without feeling that the patients are worthless or beyond help.

(f) Therapists should be realistic, able to work with the patients' goals while accepting the constraints that are placed by the patients' abilities and by the environment.

(g) Therapists should always be ethical and moral.

Further discussion of some of these characteristics can be found in the writings of Carl Rogers (1967).

There are also certain characteristics that are important for therapists to have in specific situations. Three such situations will be discussed: the diagnostic situation, the therapy contract situation, and the treatment situation.

The diagnostic situation usually calls for a passive stance on the part of therapists. The professionals in this situation are mainly observers—they look and listen, allowing the patients as much control and being as unintrusive as possible so that patients are free to behave in their most characteristic way.

During the setting of the therapeutic contract, professionals move from the observer's role to that of negotiator. They still have to be able to listen to what clients want, but now they can be more intrusive, pointing out the reality factors involved. Therapists usually know already what they would like to offer, so the job at this point is to sell as much of the package as they can to the patient. As a result, at times it helps to be engaging and even a little flattering. It also helps to be enthusiastic about the proposed treatment.

The behaviors that are useful during the treatment situation are impossible to generalize. They vary according to the personality style of the patient (see section V.A) and the specific problems and treatment goals.

V.E.   HANDLING DIFFICULT SITUATIONS

In our work with emotionally disturbed individuals, we often have to face difficult situations. The goal of the professional is to respond to those situations in a way that is effective in handling the problem and therapeutically designed to decrease the amount of psychopathology in the patient. The following are situations that are often found troublesome. Some tips on handling them are given. When the therapist becomes more sophisticated, he or she may wish to respond in a different manner, after taking into account the patient's personality style and psychopathology.

Personal Questions

Personal questions involving the therapist's training or professional position may be handled as questions about treatment (to be discussed). Two issues have to be considered in handling other personal questions:

(a) Whether or not the therapist should give the information requested.

(b) Whether or not the therapist should explore with the patient the reason for asking the question.

To decide on whether or not the information requested should be given, the therapist should have some idea regarding the patient's goal. Some personal questions are asked by individuals who feel nervous and vulnerable in the therapeutic relationship. Knowing something about the therapist may make the patient more at ease, which may or may not be part of the treatment plan. Other times, personal questions are asked as a way of gaining attention or control. In these cases the therapist has to evaluate whether allowing the maneuver is in keeping with the treatment plan. Personal questions asked in the spirit of being intrusive, bizarre, or obnoxious should not be answered. The same applies to requests for information that will be used by the patient in a pathological way. Knowing the person's personality style and history may help to determine why the patient is asking the question. In some cases answering a personal question may prove to be antitherapeutic. If so, the incident may be seen as a situation in which something was learned about the patient rather than as a "big mistake."

When the therapist decides that the answer should not be given, he or she basically responds by guiding the patient in another direction. This can be done by:

(a) Introducing another issue (e.g., "You look better today. How are you feeling?").

(b) Exploring the patient's motivation for asking the question.

(c) Talking about the goals to be accomplished during the session (e.g., "The purpose of our talking together is to see how your problems can be helped. Let's not waste time on other issues.").

(d) Talking about the therapist's reactions to the question (e.g., "You know, I am feeling uncomfortable. I really don't want to answer that kind of question.").

Finally, the therapist should decide whether or not to explore with the patient the reasons for asking. This issue should be decided on the basis of the treatment plan and independently of whether or not to offer an answer to the question.

Questions about the Treatment

Questions about the treatment should be answered in the most truthful and objective fashion possible. These questions involve the "rights of the consumer." A therapist's belief that the information would not help the patient cannot negate his or her human rights to have the information available.

Questions about Another Patient

Questions about another patient should not be answered because they involve the right to privacy of the other patient. Of the possible ways of avoiding the answer, I prefer explaining truthfully to the patient that I cannot talk about another patient without his or her consent.

Negative Material about Another Professional

Occasionally a therapist faces a situation in which a patient brings up negative material about another professional. Usually the best response is to listen and accept the patient's feelings as such, without being defensive but without agreeing in any way. The therapist should avoid siding with the patient against the other professional, most particularly if the other person is a member of the staff at the same facility.

Sexual Advances

When sexual advances are made by a patient, the therapist's job is to reject the idea without rejecting the patient or jeopardizing the therapeutic relationship. One technique that I have found useful is to discuss the role of a therapist. This discussion usually provides a good reason for the therapist's disinterest without humiliating the patient.

Hostility

Professionals working with severely disturbed individuals commonly encounter a patient who is hostile. This type of problem usually starts with the patient being verbally abusive. A physical attack can often be prevented with the following moves:

- (a) Keep extremely calm at all times. Pay attention to your own feelings and try to remain as relaxed as possible. Speak softly and gently when addressing the patient.
- (b) Have someone call for help if this is not already available (other professionals, guards, or police).
- (c) Try to isolate the patient. This can be done by asking the patient to come to an office to discuss the problem or asking all nonprofessionals in the area to move away. (This move keeps arousing stimuli from reaching the patient and protects others.)
- (d) Listen to the patient, allowing him or her to vent anger verbally. Try not to interrupt, and avoid confrontation if possible.

If limits have to be set, follow these recommendations:

(a) Get as much help as possible. (This "show of force" often prevents the need to take physical action.)

(b) Tell the patient what the limits are in a calm and gentle voice but with assurance and firmness (e.g., "Mr. Smith, I understand that you are upset, and I am here to help. However, we cannot allow physical violence. Try to control yourself so that we don't have to place you in restraints.") Do not tell the patient that you are going to do something that you cannot do.

(c) Do not attempt physical restraints without enough help to do the job safely, unless the patient is going to seriously harm himself or herself or others at that moment.

(d) If physical restraints are necessary and enough help is available, form a circle around the patient. Those at the patient's back should start the restraining process by holding the patient's arms. At that point, those in front should hold the feet and everyone should pull, lifting the patient off the floor.

(e) Use the minimal amount of force necessary to restrain the patient.

Suicidal Calls or Threats

The method prescribed for handling suicidal or threatening calls is to be warm and friendly and to encourage the patient to continue talking. An attempt should be made to evaluate the risk involved (see section VIII.A) and to obtain an address from the caller. If the risk is imminent, the police or fire department should be called. An effort should be made, however, to obtain the patient's permission to call for help, and an attempt should be made to establish a contract with the patient that he or she will not do anything before help arrives.

Therapist's Strong Feelings

A patient may sometimes evoke strong feelings in the therapist. Sometimes these feelings are the type that would be felt by any therapist handling the patient (an insulting or overcontrolling patient may tend to evoke anger or fear, an anxious patient tends to make the therapist anxious, a sexy patient may be found sexually arousing). At other times these feelings may be the therapist's own personal reaction to the patient due to personal past experiences (countertransference). Although acting on the therapist's feelings sometimes may be therapeutic, most often it is not. Appropriate handling requires, first, an awareness of the personal feelings and, second, the ability to behave in a therapeutic manner in spite of the personal feelings. These situations are probably the most difficult, but perhaps they are also the situations that differentiate the outstanding therapist from the rest.

VI Treatment Methods

VI.A. PERSONALITY-BASED SUPPORTIVE THERAPY

"Supportive therapy" is the kind of treatment designed to reduce the amount of friction that the individual has with the environment without making any demands on the individual to change. In its purest form, this mode of therapy is usually prescribed for an individual who is thought not to have the resources needed for a meaningful change, at least at the time the therapy is implemented. Often what is meant by "supportive therapy" is simply that the therapist will be making an effort to be understanding, conciliatory, sympathetic, compassionate, and nonconfrontative. If those attributes are present in the relationship, it would generally be thought that the relationship would feel comfortable to the client and would contribute to tension reduction. In spite of the merits of that general approach to therapy, the prescription of the same mode of interaction for every patient can be criticized as unduly simplistic and as failing to recognize the uniqueness of the individual and the level of sophistication that therapists are capable of.

One way of refining the system is by considering the client's personality style. Knowing the basic assumptions of life that the individual holds and the cluster of traits that make up the client's personality structure allows the practitioner to set up an interpersonal environment during the session that is designed to be experienced by the client as ego-syntonic and congenial to his or her own way of thinking.

Table 15 notes some of the interpersonal characteristics that theoretically would lead to a supportive therapeutic experience with the different personality styles. Note the flexibility that this additional level of sophistication allows. For any particular type of intervention—for instance, confrontation—consideration of the personality style allows the practitioner to avoid such interventions at all costs with some individuals (i.e., avoidant or dependent clients) while using it with others (i.e., competitives). With most of our clients, the issues become more complex than the table would lead us to believe, since most people have a combination of more than one personality style. Thus, the therapist has to mix and integrate the recommendations that are given in order to do justice to most clients in treatment.

Especially in the case of individuals whose personality traits are extreme or rigid and who may be considered to have a personality disorder, care should be taken not to emphasize ego-syntonic recommendations to the point of fostering further pathology. For the supportive relationship to

TABLE 15. Supportive Interventions for the Different Personality Styles

Style	Supportive Attributes
1. Schizoid	Accept interpersonal distance
	Problem solve in practical matters
	Do not emphasize insight
	Do not emphasize relationships
2. Avoidant	Reassure
	Be careful with negative interpretations
	Be relaxed
3. Dependent	Be dominant
	Be protective
4. Histrionic	Allow patient to be center of attention
	Be emotionally demonstrative
5. Narcissistic	Allow patient to be dominant
	Be careful with negative interpretations
6. Competitive	Accept competitive assumption
	Show how patient is not competing well in terms of his or her psychological functioning
	Be firm when limits are tested
7. Compulsive	Be on time
	Be organized
	Accept hierarchical view of the world
8. Passive-aggressive/explosive	As much as possible, do not tell patient what to do (any controls will be used as an issue by the patient)
	Tolerate and interpret moods

remain beneficial, the therapist has to operate at the same level as the individual, so that the relationship is comfortable without being antitherapeutic. With a dependent individual, for instance, if the therapist is to take responsibility for things that the client can handle, the interventions could be seen as encouraging the individual to become more dependent than he or she already is.

VI.B. FUNDAMENTALS OF INDIVIDUAL THERAPY

Individual therapy usually has one or more of the following goals:

(a) To increase the level of understanding that patients have about themselves or the environment.

(b) To establish a relationship that allows patients to work through childhood conflicts.

(c) To help patients change themselves or the environment so that life becomes less stressful.

Any of these goals are appropriate for individual therapy, singly or in combination with another form of treatment. However, these goals should be in keeping with the overall treatment plan as discussed in Chapter V.

To increase the level of understanding that patients have about themselves and the environment, therapists must encourage patients to explore this area and help patients to gain psychological insight. This is done in different ways by the different schools of therapy. A discussion of the different styles is beyond the scope of the present work. Some references will be given with the discussion of specific therapeutic techniques below. A survey done by Katz and Hennessey (1981) led to the following list of recommended references, presented in their order of ranking:

Fromm-Reichmann, F. (1950). *Principles of intensive psychotherapy.* Chicago: University of Chicago Press.

Greenson, R. R. (1967). *The technique and practice of psychoanalysis.* New York: International Universities Press.

Wolberg, L. R. (1967). *The technique of psychotherapy* (2nd ed.). New York: Grune & Stratton.

Corsini, R. J. (1973). *Current psychotherapies.* Itasca, IL: Peacock.

Rogers, C. R. (1951). *Client-centered therapy.* Boston: Houghton Mifflin.

Singer, E. (1965). *Key concepts in psychotherapy.* New York: Random House.

Sullivan, H. S. (1956). *The psychiatric interview.* New York: Norton.

Bergin, A. E., & Garfield, S. L. (Eds.). (1971). *Handbook of psychotherapy and behavior change: An empirical analysis.* New York: John Wiley.

Colby, K. M. (1951). *A primer for psychotherapists.* New York: Ronald Press.

Fabricant, B., & Barron, J. (1977). *To enjoy is to live: Psychotherapy explained.* Chicago: Nelson Hall.

Frank, J. D. (1973). *Persuasion and healing* (rev. ed.). Baltimore: Johns Hopkins University Press.

Goldfried, M. R., & Davison, G. C. (1976). *Clinical behavior therapy.* New York: Holt, Rinehart and Winston.

Haley, J. (1963). *Strategies of psychotherapy.* New York: Grune & Stratton.

Rogers, C. R. (1961). *On becoming a person: A therapist's view of psychotherapy.* Boston: Houghton Mifflin.

Additional recommendations are:

Horowitz, M., Marmar, C., Krupnick, J., Wilner, N., Kaltreider, N., & Wallerstein, R. (1984). *Personality styles and brief psychotherapy.* New York: Basic Books.

Langs, R. (1982). *Psychotherapy: A basic text.* New York: Jason Aronson.

Lazarus, A. A. (1976). *Multimodal behavior therapy.* New York: Springer Publishing Company.

Strupp, H. H., & Binder, J. L. (1984). *Psychotherapy in a new key: A guide to time-limited dynamic psychotherapy.* New York: Basic Books.

Once patients have an understanding of how friction is created between themselves and the environment, the changes that are necessary in order to reduce the friction should be evident. Often these changes follow the increased understanding without any difficulty. When the changes do not follow, one of the following factors is probably present:

(a) The change constitutes an approach-avoidance conflict: some negative aspects will result from the change so that the patient is trying to avoid it.

(b) The change involves habitual behavioral patterns that the patient finds difficult to break.

In an approach-avoidance situation, the conflict can be real or imagined. If the result of change that the patient is trying to avoid is real, the patient can be helped to understand the situation clearly and to make an existential decision about it, accepting the consequences. If the conflict is imagined, the attempt should be made to determine its origins and work through the feelings involved.

If habitual patterns have to be changed, a behavioral approach is often helpful. The method involves determining what stimulus leads to the undesirable response, what other responses are appropriate, and what system of reinforcements can be used to change the association.

When the goal of therapy is understanding or change, the resulting relationship is — by necessity — less supportive. When the goal is to increase understanding, the therapy may be more threatening because the person has to face some things about himself or herself that are negative and that have been defended against in the past. When the goal is personality change the therapeutic behaviors indicated are sometimes the opposite of what was recommended for supportive therapy, so that the relationship is perceived as uncomfortable by the patient.

When the goal of therapy is to increase the level of understanding or to produce some personality change, the issue of the amount of change also has to be decided. The term *intensive psychotherapy* is used when the goal is to create substantial changes in the patient. For these changes to come about, in most cases the therapy sessions must be quite frequent and the therapeutic relationship becomes very involved. Often the relationship is so involved that the mere vacationing of the therapist is difficult for the patient to handle.

VI.C. FUNDAMENTALS OF GROUP THERAPY

There are many approaches to group therapy that are considered today to be individual therapy in groups. They pursue basically the same goals listed for individual therapy by allotting time to the different patients in one way or another. The differences in the goal chosen or the mode used to reach it are beyond the scope of the present work, but the student can review them in the book by Kaplan and Sadock (1971).

Individual therapy in groups can be of great value. However, the field of group therapy seems to be gradually unifying behind the group process model. Research has repeatedly found this model to be of value (e.g., Yalom, 1985) and it involves a different concept of group work. For users of the group process model, the goal of group therapy is to create a sense of cohesiveness among the group members. Once this basic goal is accepted, it becomes a guiding force that can be used to answer all the other issues that concern group therapy. Some of those issues will now be discussed.

Membership

One of the jobs of a group therapist is to recruit and choose the members of the group. In doing so, he or she may use the following rules:

(a) A member should be an individual who has an emotional problem which may be helped by the experience of membership in a cohesive and accepting group. It is easy to see, for instance, how patients with interpersonal anxiety or social withdrawal or patients with feelings of unworthiness or an inability to trust others may be helped by this method. On the other hand, this may not be an appropriate treatment for an individual who has marital difficulties. A member should not be assigned to a group simply because there is room. It is the responsibility of the therapist to evaluate the patient's needs and make sure that it is feasible to think of the group as a solution to at least some of his or her problems.

(b) A member should be an individual who is compatible with the other group members. Although groups tend to be tolerant and accept a fair amount of diversity, the therapist should try not to choose individuals who are going to be very different from the rest. Variables to be considered are the person's intellectual abilities, interests, socioeconomic class, education, and severity of psychopathology. Other variables like sex, race, age, and sexual orientation may also be important, depending on the individual. Errors in matching result in individuals who never quite become part of the group and often drop out after a short time.

Administrative Duties

The second task that a group therapist has is administering the group. This usually involves deciding on a time when the group can meet, setting limits of acceptable behavior for members of the group, and keeping progress notes on the different members.

Frequency of Intervention

In general, the group therapist tries to have members communicate as much as possible with each other. The goal, therefore, is to minimize the therapist's interventions, since they take away time in which the members could be interacting with one another. The exception to this rule is when the therapist feels that intervention will improve group cohesiveness.

Types of Intervention

Group cohesiveness is improved through interventions that:
(a) Allow the group to understand one member better.
(b) Help the members of the group relate better to one another.
(c) Help the members of the group see themselves as belonging to the group and see the group as a unit.
Most helpful in achieving the goal of improving group cohesiveness are interventions that deal with group process. For further information on recognizing and dealing with group process, the book by Whitaker and Lieberman (1965) is recommended.

Mode of Intervention

Whenever possible, the therapist should make a point through a group member rather than making the point by him or herself. For instance, if a member has been talking for some time about a topic that is boring to the rest of the members, the therapist should look around the room for a member who looks bored and ask what he or she is feeling at this time. If this fails, the therapist could turn to another member and ask what reactions he or she had to what the first member was saying. Some group therapists feel that a point that cannot be brought out by involving a group member is not worth bringing out. Although there are certainly exceptions to that rule, it does not seem a bad rule of thumb to keep in mind.

Use of Co-therapist

Groups are often run by two therapists, and this practice seems very beneficial. It is important, however, that the therapists themselves are compatible and that they run the group with the same goals in mind. Often this type of teamwork can only be achieved after some time during which the therapists meet outside the group to discuss the group sessions.

A good book on group therapy that espouses these principles is the book by Yalom (1985).

VI.D.   FUNDAMENTALS OF FAMILY THERAPY

Family therapy may be the treatment of choice when:
 (a) The problem involves the way family members relate to one another or is assumed to be the result of a pathological family system.
 (b) It is possible to motivate all the family members concerned to work toward changes in the family system.

Probably the most important issue in family therapy is how the family handles control (the decision-making process). Four options are possible:
 (a) The Overadequate-Underadequate Family has one member with all controls. This member is seen as dominant and superior while others play a submissive role and accept his or her decisions. The play *A Doll's House* by Henrik Ibsen provides a good description of this type of relationship.
 (b) The United Front Family involves a system in which no one makes the decisions. Members portray themselves as being in total agreement and reaching decisions in common, but they usually do not feel that they can express any disagreement.
 (c) The Conflictual Family relationships involve constant quarrelling between family members. Everyone wants to have control of the decision-making process and argues frequently on issues in an attempt to establish that control. An example of this type of relationship is seen in the play *Who's Afraid of Virginia Woolf* by Edward Albee.
 (d) The Shared Control Family has different members controlling different aspects at different times.

The different family systems are made up of individuals with particular personality styles. Often their personality styles fit well into the system. For instance, an overadequate-underadequate system may be made up of a narcissistic husband and a dependent wife (see Chapter I); in a conflictual family there may be a histrionic and a passive-aggressive member.

There is a tendency among professionals to look at one of the control systems as being superior to the rest (the shared control family). Although research has supported this contention, I have seen families that worked reasonably well that functioned under one of the other systems. I feel it is preferable to think of each system as having some advantages and some disadvantages. The overadequate-underadequate system, for instance, may be more effective than the rest at times of crisis. During a crisis the shared control system may not be efficient enough and could easily lapse into a conflictual system. The view supported here, therefore, is that the type of system used is not itself a problem unless it is very extreme. Rather, family pathology can be defined as ineffective family functioning, regardless of the system used.

Family difficulties may be related to a specific issue or may arise out of friction within the system. Difficulties that are issue related are differences of opinion that the family has not worked through but that do not carry any control implications. In a system that is functioning effectively, these issues do not become pathological if the family is given the opportunity to work them out.

Family pathology usually arises out of difficulties within the system. These difficulties may be of two types:

(a) Discomfort of one or more family members as a result of being forced to play a role in the system that does not agree with their present personality style. An example is an overadequate-underadequate system in which an underadequate person has become, through taking a job outside the family, less submissive.

(b) Pathological behavior of one or more members who have developed the pathology as a way of fitting into the system. An example is the child in a conflictual family who started flunking in school when her mother began telling her father that his excessive drinking was affecting the children.

In order to do family therapy effectively, one first must evaluate all members who are judged to be important to the family system. At the end of this evaluation, the therapist should have a clear idea of what system the family uses and what personality styles the different members have.

Once the evaluation is finished, the therapist has to develop a plan of action. In the case of the discomfort of a member who is forced to play a role he or she does not want to play, the family treatment plan may be to:

(a) Help the family member experiencing the discomfort to be more at ease with this role in the family, or

(b) Help the system to change so that the person is no longer forced to play a distasteful role.

In the case of pathological behavior that a family member develops as a way of fitting into the system, the family treatment plan would be to:

(a) Help the family member find a nonpathological way of fitting into the system, or

(b) Change the family system so that it does not encourage the pathological behavior.

The family treatment plan is put into effect by involving the whole family. Real changes are usually accomplished only when the family arrives at their own idea of what needs to be changed and their own way to change it. The job of the therapist is to guide the family in their work rather than to do any work for them. This task is easily done in the case of discomfort with a role: the therapist should encourage discussion of the issue of the discomfort until the family faces the problem. Then the therapist can guide them in their effort to find solutions. In the case of pathological behaviors that result from the system, the task is often harder to accomplish. However, the method should be similar: encourage the family to talk about themselves until the problem is clear; then help the family to find solutions.

Recommended references are:

Ackerman, N. W. (1966). *Treating the troubled family.* New York: Basic Books.
Bowen, M. (1978). *Family therapy in clinical practice.* New York: Jason Aronson.
Ferber, A., Mendelsohn, M., & Napier, A. (1972). *The book of family therapy.* New York: Science House.
Gurman, A. S., & Kniskern, D. P. (Eds.). (1981). *Handbook of family therapy.* New York: Brunner/Mazel.
Haley, J., & Hoffman, L. (1967). *Techniques of family therapy.* New York: Basic Books.

VI.E. SPECIFIC THERAPEUTIC TECHNIQUES

The specific therapeutic techniques that follow come from many different schools of therapy. In some instances they were proposed as one among many possible techniques by the originators. In other cases the given technique was used as the only therapeutic procedure. I recommend a problem-oriented view in which a particular technique is carefully selected to accomplish a given goal in the patient's treatment.

Some of these techniques also have a diagnostic use. The descriptions below, however, will address only the therapeutic value of the procedures.

Assertiveness Training

This technique was designed to increase assertiveness in individuals who appear to be unduly submissive. The main ideas are to:
(a) Make clients aware of their rights.
(b) Encourage clients to stand up for their rights.
(c) Rehearse ways in which clients can stand up for their rights without being unduly abrasive.
For further information see Cotler and Guerra (1976).

Aversive Conditioning

This technique is based on the idea that if undesired behaviors are associated with repulsive or aversive stimuli, the client will lose attraction for that behavior. Prevalent examples are the induction of vomiting in alcoholics right after ingestion of alcohol, and having a smoker smoke only in a repulsive or aversive place. Imagery has also been used productively in developing aversive associations. For further information see Yates (1970).

Behavioral Assignments

This technique is used when:
(a) The therapist feels that it is constructive for the client to be working on some issue before the next session.
(b) The next logical step in a therapeutic progress with regard to some problem is something that should be done outside of the therapy sessions.

Examples are having a client make a list of all the advantages and disadvantages of making a decision about which the client is conflicted, and having an isolated and withdrawn client take a small step toward less isolation or withdrawal.

Bibliotherapy

Patients who are academically oriented may be asked to read some literature that will enhance their cognitive understanding of the problem. Almost any professional book may be used for this purpose as long as it is related to the patient's problem. A book on general understanding of psycho-dynamics may also be appropriate. Be sure to allow some time for discussion of the reading material; sometimes clients misinterpret what they read in ways that may be antitherapeutic.

Confrontation

This technique is useful mainly when symptoms are being denied or minimized. Denial is particularly likely to be used by people with substance abuse disorders, or individuals with a narcissistic personality style or a sociopathic or borderline personality disorder. In the treatment of these individuals, therefore, confrontation is often an important part of the therapy. By means of confrontation, the client can be guided to face his or her resistance so that the therapeutic process can continue. It is important to keep in mind that this procedure works only so long as the therapist is perceived as remaining on the same side of the fence as the client. This can be achieved by:
(a) Avoiding a confrontation until a good relationship is established with the client (the timing of the confrontation can be important).
(b) Reminding the client that the confrontation is only undertaken in the interest of helping with his or her problems.

A client who perceives the therapist as an adversary will use all of his or her energy to fight the therapist, and the goal of the confrontation will not be achieved.

Desensitization

This technique was devised for clients who have phobic fears or apprehensions. Classical conditioning provides its theoretical basis. More specifically, desensitization attempts to associate thoughts of the feared stimulus with a relaxed mood. First, a hierarchy is constructed with situations that constitute increasing degrees of fear. For example, for a client who fears elevators, level 100 may be being in a closed elevator, level 75 may be coming into a building knowing that an elevator will have to be taken, level 50 may be standing in a small room but one that can be left, level 25 perhaps would be planning to do an errand on the following day in a building that has elevators, and so forth. The client is then helped to relax (using techniques described under Relaxation Techniques). Once relaxed, the client is asked to imagine vividly a situation that arouses a low level of anxiety. The moment the client feels apprehensive, he or she is to signal the therapist, to stop imagining the scene, and to get into a relaxed mood once more. This procedure is repeated until no anxiety is felt. At this point, the imagery is changed to the next situation in the previously constructed hierarchy. For further information see Wolpe (1958).

Empty Chair Technique

The empty chair is a Gestalt strategy designed to have the client express and experience feelings toward an absent individual as vividly as possible. The client is strongly encouraged to imagine that the absent person is sitting on a chair, and is then encouraged to talk to that person and express all of his or her feelings. Descriptions of the technique can be found in Perls (1969).

Group Exercises

The repertoire of group games or exercises is too extensive to describe in the present work. The purpose of the exercises is to promote insight or expression of feelings among group members. The exercises are especially helpful since the feelings evoked are often toward another member of the group, so they can be worked through within the group context. I tend to use group exercises only when the group is not being productive. Most of the benefit of such exercises is derived from the discussion that follows them, so time should be allowed for this discussion. A good book in this area is Morris and Cinnamon (1975).

Hypnosis

This procedure involves working with clients in ways that make them increasingly susceptible to suggestions. Once they are felt to be ready, therapeutic suggestions for change are made. Prevalent uses of hypnosis are to:
  (a) Decrease the subjective experience of pain.
  (b) Decrease or extinguish a particular symptom.
  (c) Help clients break a habit such as smoking.
The specifics in the use of this technique are beyond the scope of the present work. The reader is referred to Erickson, Rossi, and Rossi, (1976).

Interpretations

This technique is used to make the client aware of a link between a previous experience and a present assumption, feeling, or behavior. It is well known that the timing of interpretations is very important. For an interpretation to be successful, the client has to:

(a) Be very aware of both the previous experience and the present assumptions, feelings, or behaviors in question.

(b) Be in an accepting mood, in other words, able to at least hear, if not accept, what the therapist is about to suggest.

Further discussion can be found in Chessick (1974), Fromm-Reichmann (1950), Greenson (1967), Langs (1982), and Strupp and Binder, (1984).

Paradoxical Instructions

A paradoxical intention involves prescribing the symptom with the hidden goal of extinguishing it. An example would be to tell a compulsive patient that instead of taking five showers a day, he is to rearrange his life so as to take ten. For the procedure to work well, it must be done with complete seriousness and sincerity. If the patient complains, the therapist should use the same arguments and fears that the client uses to support the behavior. I recommend the use of this technique with patients who are inclined to sabotage treatment. This often includes clients with a compulsive or a passive-aggressive personality style who feel that they have to be in control, as well as clients with strong vested interests in holding on to their pathology. Further information can be obtained from Haley (1976).

Rational Disputation

Albert Ellis feels that individuals often produce the wrong behavior because they hold erroneous assumptions about the world. A rational disputation involves a rational demonstration that the assumption the client holds is wrong. For example, the overly shy individual may be unable to call for a date because of fear of rejection. Ellis would argue that this individual is assuming that being rejected is a terrible event, and he would try to convince the client that everyone, in fact, is rejected many times in his life. The technique is particularly recommended with clients who tend to value very highly the cognitive or rational aspect of themselves. This may be particularly true in the case of compulsive individuals. For further information see Ellis and Grieger (1977) or Beck, Rush, Shaw, and Emery (1979).

Reflexive Explorations

Reflexive explorations are statements in which the therapist rephrases what the client has said. When done well, the rephrasing adds meaning to the client's words and encourages the client to go on exploring his or her feelings. An example is the following interaction:

C: I had a very hard time when my wife left me.
T: Yes, I can see by your expression that you still have a lot of feelings about it.

Notice that the therapist is adding his or her perception of the client's present state and leaving the comment open-ended in a way that encourages the client to continue. This is an extremely useful technique that can be used frequently. However, it can also be overused. Its goal is to explore and make clients aware of their feelings; the reader should keep this in mind and not use the technique when this goal is not being pursued. Further help can be obtained from Rogers (1951).

Reinforcement

The technique of giving positive or negative reinforcement to clients is so common that some behaviorists have claimed that other techniques are simply different contexts in which reinforcement is given. Whether or not this is the case, the importance of responding appropriately to therapeutic gains or losses cannot be overemphasized. There are occasions when a therapist will want to work out with the patient a system of reinforcements with specific criteria that have to be met. This may be particularly useful with:
(a) Very regressed patients who need a very concrete system to motivate them into any kind of activity.
(b) Sociopathic or borderline individuals who may be constantly attempting to "push the limits" of acceptable behavior.
More information about systems for schedules of reinforcement can be found in Levis (1970).

Relaxation Techniques

Jacobson described in his book on anxiety and tension control (1964) a procedure for muscle relaxation. The procedure involves paying attention to the muscles in one part of the body while contracting and relaxing them. Attention is then moved to another part of the body, where the process is repeated. Eventually several parts may be contracted or relaxed at the same time while the attention of the subject continues to be focused on how the muscles feel. Also involved are suggestions that the subject is feeling completely relaxed, suggestions that may have a hypnotic-like effect. For readers who want to use this technique, a useful set of audiotapes is made by Arnold A. Lazarus and produced by I.D.I., 166 E. Superior St., Chicago, IL.

Role Playing

This procedure involves having clients play themselves or other persons in some important interaction of their lives. Goals may be:
  (a) To have clients put themselves in the shoes of another person and realize how that person was feeling.
  (b) To allow histrionic clients to be the center of attention in a productive way.
  (c) To have clients rehearse a particular role that they will have to play in real life in the future.
  (d) To help withdrawn clients interact with others in a highly structured setting.
The technique can be done in a group where the other group members also participate in the acting. For further information the reader is referred to Leveton (1977).

Self-monitoring

This procedure consists of having clients keep careful track of some data that are considered to have therapeutic importance. Examples are feelings of clients toward their work in the course of a week, marital arguments, drinks taken, food ingested, or body weight. Self-monitoring may be done to:
  (a) Have the client pay attention to the data in question.
  (b) Create a system by which reinforcement can be obtained both externally (e.g., from the therapist) and internally (e.g., a feeling of accomplishment).
  (c) Produce some insight (e.g., that the client is drinking too much).

Transactional Analysis

This technique involves the analysis of an interpersonal pattern of behavior that clients have established for themselves. As Berne (1964) pointed out, often this pattern of behavior has its own reward, so that clients get into a vicious cycle that is hard to break. In analyzing the interpersonal pattern, the therapist may hope to clarify the role that clients are playing and to have them decide what they have to do in order to break the vicious cycle. The recommended reading is the work by Berne.

Thought Control

This procedure involves teaching clients to focus their attention on some sort of imagery when distracting, obsessive, or disturbing thoughts come to mind. This method can be best used:
  (a) With individuals who are disturbed by particular thoughts, such as obsessive patients.
  (b) In the management of patients with chronic pain.

VI.F FUNDAMENTALS OF DRUG TREATMENT

The importance of drugs in the treatment of emotional disorders cannot be denied. As a result, psychologists find themselves frequently dealing with individuals who take psychotropic medications or having to evaluate individuals for possible medication referrals. Some familiarity with the available drugs and their effects is of great value in making these assessments.

The contraindications for a particular drug appearing in the tables later in this chapter are subject to medical evaluation and are not always sufficient reason for not using the drug. Whenever the psychologist knows that one of these contraindications is present, however, this information should be given to the consulting psychiatrist.

Most of the possible side effects are seldom seen. An exception is the extrapyramidal symptoms frequently seen with the use of major tranquilizers or tricyclic antidepressants. These side effects may be suppressed with the use of antiparkinsonian agents. These extrapyramidal symptoms may include:

(a) Akathisia, or restlessness with inability to sleep, a compulsion to walk, and an inability to be still.

(b) Dyskinesias and dystonias, which may include jerking or spastic movements, upward deviation of the eyes, spasms of the neck, and, in severe cases, spasms of the mouth and pharynx with inability to speak or swallow.

(c) Parkinsonian syndrome or parkinsonism, which includes tremors, muscular rigidity of limbs and face (masklike facies), and slowness or scarcity of movements, with lack of associated movements such as arm swing.

The extrapyramidal effects tend to disappear over time. As a result, the usual technique is to add the antiparkinsonian drug when the symptoms appear and plan to reduce and discontinue this medication four months thereafter. At that point the symptoms may not reappear, even when the individual continues to take the psychotropic drug. This procedure encourages discontinuing medications that the patient no longer needs.

About 5% of the patients who take antipsychotic medications for some period of time develop tardive dyskinesia. This syndrome is characterized by a sucking-like puckering of the lips; chewing, licking, or pursing movements of the tongue or mouth; or choreiform movements of the extremities. Tardive dyskinesia is irreversible in most cases, and there is no known treatment. If the condition is detected, the drug should be discontinued if at all possible. If the risk of relapse is too great, thioridazine (Mellaril), which is least likely to produce this disorder, may be used after informed consent has been obtained.

A number of drugs may induce psychiatric reactions or complicate and aggravate previously existing conditions. The therapist should consult reference works or a physician whenever there is any question about a medication that the patient is taking.

Consulting a psychiatrist appropriately is a bit of an art. For the psychologist this involves:

(a) Passing along the information that the psychiatrist will need. This information may include a psychiatric and medication history, present and past medical illnesses of importance, the present mental status, and psychotropic medications used by the patient and his or her blood relatives and their response to them.

(b) Approaching the situation as one professional consulting another. On the one hand, the psychologist is not asking for a personal favor. On the other hand, the psychiatrist is not a prescription-writing machine but, rather, a highly trained professional who has much to contribute to the treatment of the patient.

(c) Having realistic expectations. In order to be legally protected and to ensure that the right medication and dosage are used, the physician has to have a certain amount of contact with the patient. Psychiatrists differ in the amount of contact that they feel is needed. The patient and the psychologist also have to be comfortable with the amount of involvement that the psychiatrist intends to have.

(d) Making an effort to find psychiatrists with whom the psychologist feels comfortable collaborating. The situation in which one of the professionals involved has a strong dislike for the other or does not see the other as competent is not conducive to a good collaborative treatment plan. Great effort must be made so that any problems in the relationship between the two professionals do not jeopardize the treatment of the patient.

TABLE 16. Abbreviations Used in Medication Prescriptions

Term	Meaning
pc	after meals
hs	at bedtime
qd	once a day
qh	once an hour
bid	twice a day
tid	three times a day
qid	four times a day
prn	as needed
stat	to be given immediately
po	by mouth
im	intramuscularly (by injection into the muscle)
iv	intravenously (by injection into the vein)
gr	gram
mg	milligram

Further information about medications can be obtained from a recent edition of the Physician's Desk Reference (published by Medical Economics), commonly called the PDR, or from a recent edition of the American Medical Association's *Drug Evaluations.*

Table 16 (on p. 140) shows the abbreviations that are commonly associated with the prescription of medications. Tables 17 through 22 give basic information for each of the different groups of psychotropic medications.

TABLE 17. Sedative Hypnotic Agents

Other name: "Sleepers"

Actions
1. Sedation, induction of sleep (for brief, intermittent use)
2. Alleviation of anxiety before surgery

Side effects
1. Dizziness, drowsiness, confusion
2. Nausea, vomiting, "upset stomach"
3. "Hangover" with morning headaches
4. High potential for abuse and dependency

Contraindications
1. Pregnancy
2. Hazardous occupation that requires alertness
3. Porphyria (with barbiturates only)

Delay: Varies; see below

Drug Type	Trade Name	Generic Name	Specific Actions	Dosage (mg)
Barbiturates	Seconal	Secobarbital	Quick action	100–200
	Amytal	Amobarbital		30–200
	Tuinal	Secobarbital & amobarbital		50–200
	Luminal	Phenobarbital	Long acting	15–120
	Mebaral	Mephobarbital		32–100
	Nembutal	Pentobarbital	Quick action	100–200
Benzodiazepines	Dalmane	Flurazepam		15–30
	Halcion	Triazolam	No hangover	0.25–0.50
	Restoril	Temazepam		15–30
Other	Doriden	Glutethimide	Very addictive	250–500
	Noctec	Chloral hydrate	Quick action	250–1000
	Noludar	Methyprylon		50–400
	Placidyl	Ethchlorvynol		200–750

TABLE 18. Minor Tranquilizers

Other names: Antianxiety agents, anxiolytics

Actions
1. Reduction of anxiety during periods of acute stress
2. Relief of symptoms of withdrawal from alcohol
3. Decrease of motor activity
4. Muscle relaxation

Side effects
1. Lethargy, drowsiness, dizziness
2. Decreased coordination
3. Nausea, constipation
4. Tendency toward abuse and dependency
5. Menstrual irregularities (rare)
7. Jaundice (rare)
8. Bone marrow suppression (rare)

Contraindications
1. Pregnancy
2. Patient less than 6 years of age
3. Hazardous occupation requiring alertness and coordination
4. Acute narrow angle glaucoma
5. Use of alcohol

Delay: One hour

Drug Type	Trade Name	Generic Name	Indications/ Specific Actions	Dosage (mg per day)
Benzodiazepines	Ativan	Lorazepam	Moderate	2–6
	Centrax	Prazepam	depression	20–60
	Librium or	Chlordiazep-	Alcohol withdrawal	30–300
	Libritabs	oxide		20–100
	Paxipam	Halazepam		80–160
	Serax	Oxazepam		30–60
	Tranxene	Clorazepate	Alcohol withdrawal, anxiety disorder	15–60 7.5–30
	Valium	Diazepam	Alcohol withdrawal, muscle relaxant	10–60 4–40
	Xanax	Alprazolam	Depression	0.25–4
Azaspiro- decanediones	BuSpar	Buspirone	Less sedating, less abuse potential	10–60
Carbamates	Equanil	Meprobamate	Higher potential for addiction & with- drawal seizures	400–1600
	Miltown	Meprobamate		
Diphenylmethane	Atarax	Hydroxyzine		75–200
	Vistaril	Hydroxyzine		50–100

TABLE 19. Neuroleptics

Other names: Antipsychotic agents, major tranquilizers

Actions
1. Reduction of delusions and hallucinations
2. Ordering of the thought process
3. Reduction of tension and anxiety
4. Decrease of motor agitation

Side effects
1. Extrapyramidal symptoms (see text for description)
2. Tardive dyskinesia (see text)
3. Dryness of mouth and throat, blurred vision
4. Constipation
5. Urinary retention
6. Decrease in sexual drive, inhibition of ejaculation
7. Drop in blood pressure when standing up, dizziness, tachycardia
8. Skin rashes
9. Menstrual irregularities
10. Weight gain, occasionally weight loss
11. Jaundice
12. Lowered seizure threshold, possible convulsions

Contraindications
1. Sensitivity to neuroleptics
2. Hazardous occupation requiring alertness and coordination
3. Comatose states
4. Previous intake of large amounts of alcohol, barbiturates or narcotics

Delay: Several days

(continued)

TABLE 19. *(continued)*

Drug Type	Trade Name	Generic Name	Specific Actions/ Side Effects	Dosage (mg per day)
Butyrophenones	Haldol	Haloperidol	Side effect 1[a], low sedation	2–100
	Haldol Decanoate	Haloperidol	As above; long acting	50 mg im/wk
Dibenzoxazepines	Loxitane Daxolin	Loxapine succinate Loxapine succinate	High sedation	10–250
Indolone	Moban	Molindone HCl	Weight loss	25–400
Rauwolfia alkaloids	Serpasil	Reserpine	Sedative, hypotensive	0.25–3
Phenothiazines Aliphatic	Thorazine	Chlorpromazine	Strong sedative, hypotensive	50–1000
Propylpiperazine	Compazine	Prochlorperazine	For all:	10–40
	Permitil	Fluphenazine HCl	side effect 1[a]	0.5–10
	Prolixin	Fluphenazine HCl	low sedation	1–20
	Prolixin Decanoate	Fluphenazine decanoate	Long acting	25 mg im/2 wk
	Prolixin Enanthate	Fluphenazine enanthate	Long acting	25 im
	Repoise	Butaperazine		15–100
	Stelazine	Trifluoperazine HCl		5–30
	Trilafon	Perphenazine		12–64
Ethylpiperidine	Mellaril	Thioridazine HCl	For all:	50–800
	Quide	Piperacetazine	low side effect	10–160
	Serentil	Mesoridazine	1, 3[a]	50–400
Phenothiazine and tricyclic	Triavil Etrafon	Perphenazine & amitriptyline	Combination antipsychotic & antidepressant	Variable[b]
Thioxanthenes	Navane	Thiothixene		5–40
	Taractan	Chlorprothixene	Sedative, hypotensive	25–600

[a] Numbers refer to list above.
[b] Depends on the relative concentration of the two chemical agents.

TABLE 20. Antidepressants

Actions
1. Relief of depressive symptoms
2. Reduction of psychomotor retardation
3. Increase of motivation and optimism

Side effects
1. Dizziness, drowsiness, weakness, confusion, or stupor
2. Dryness of mouth and throat, blurred vision
3. Nausea, vomiting, constipation or diarrhea
4. Urinary disturbance
5. Drop in blood pressure when standing up
6. Tachycardia (rapid heart rate), palpitations, arrhythmia
7. Lowering of seizure threshold, convulsions
8. Accelerated psychomotor activity
9. Activation of psychotic symptoms: hallucinations, delusions
10. Insomnia
11. Weight gain or loss
12. Perspiration

Contraindications
1. Prostatic hypertrophy (with tricyclics)
2. Glaucoma (with tricyclics)
3. Recent myocardial infarction
4. Arrhythmia

Delay: Two to four weeks

(continued)

TABLE 20. *(continued)*

Drug Type	Trade Name	Generic Name	Specific Actions	Dosage (mg per day)
Dibenzoxa-zepine	Asendin	Amoxapine	Sedating	150–400
Monoamine oxidase inhibitors	Marplan	Isocarboxazid	Used mostly with pts. who have not responded to other antidepressants; require a tyramine-free diet	10–50
	Nardil	Phenelzine		15–75
	Parnate	Tranylcypromine		10–30
Tetracyclic	Ludiomil	Maprotiline		75–150
Triazolo-pyridine	Desyrel	Trazodone	For anxious pts.	150–600
Tricyclics	Adapin	Doxepin	Sedating	75–200
	Aventyl HCl	Nortriptyline		20–100
	Elavil	Amitriptyline		50–225
	Endep	Amitriptyline		75–150
Tricyclic and benzodia-zepine	Limbitrol	Amitriptyline & chlordiazepoxide	For agitated pts.	Variable[a]
	Norpramin	Desipramine		75–200
	Pamelor	Nortriptyline		75–150
	Sinequan	Doxepin	Sedating	40–200
	Surmontil	Trimipramine		75–200
	Tofranil	Imipramine		50–225
Tricyclic and phenothia-zine	Triavil Etrafon	Amitriptyline & perphenazine	For psychotic pts.	Variable[a]
	Vivactil	Protriptyline		10–60

[a] Depends on the relative concentration of the two chemicals involved.

TABLE 21. Therapeutic Agents Used in Bipolar or Schizoaffective Disorders

Actions
1. Decrease of elation and reduction of psychomotor activity in manic states
2. Increase of optimism, motivation, and psychomotor activity in depressed states

Side effects
1. Nausea, vomiting, diarrhea, or abdominal pain
2. Muscular weakness
3. Sluggish or dazed feeling
4. Thirst and excessive urination
5. Fine hand tremor
6. Intoxication produces drowsiness, tremors, slurred speech, convulsions, and coma

Must be used cautiously in cases of:
1. Thyroid deficiency (hypothyroidism)
2. Renal deficiency
3. Liver deficiency
4. Cardiovascular disease
5. Patients receiving diuretics

Delay: One to three weeks

Trade Name	Generic Name	Specifications	Dosage (mg per day)
Eskalith	Lithium carbonate	Must reach blood	300–1800
Lithane	Lithium carbonate	levels of 0.7 to 1.2	
Lithonate	Lithium carbonate	mEq/li for thera-	
Lithotabs	Lithium carbonate	peutic effect; toxic above 1.5 mEq/li	
Eskalith CR	Lithium carbonate	Slow release	
Lithobid	Lithium carbonate	Slow release	
Cibalith-S	Lithium citrate	Slow release	5 cc–30 cc
Tegretol	Carbamazepine	Also used with temporal lobe dysfunction	400–1600

Note: These medications are often used in combination with a neuroleptic or with one another, so that a patient may be taking both Tegretol and lithium, lithium and a neuroleptic, etc.

TABLE 22. Antiparkinsonian Agents

Indications
1. Parkinson disease
2. Drug-induced extrapyramidal symptoms

Actions: Relieve side effects of neuroleptics

Side effects
1. Dry mouth, blurred vision, dizziness, drowsiness
2. Urinary retention
3. Nausea, vomiting, constipation
4. Exacerbation of psychotic state

Contraindications
1. Hypersensitivity to the drug
2. Tardive dyskinesia
3. Glaucoma

Delay: About 20 minutes when injected

Drug Type	Trade Name	Generic Name	Specific Actions	Dosage (mg)
Anticholinergic	Akineton	Biperiden		2–8
	Artane	Trihexyphenidyl		2–15
	Cogentin	Benztropine		0.5–6
	Kemadrin	Procyclidine		10–20
	Disipal	Orphenadrine HCl		50–150
Other	Symmetrel	Amantadine		

VII The Clinical Record

VII.A. INTRODUCTION

Table 23, at the end of this chapter, offers a list of commonly used medical abbreviations that trainees may find helpful in understanding medical charts. Abbreviations associated with the prescription of medications were presented in Table 16, in Chapter VI.

A complete clinical record includes four parts:

(a) The data base
(b) The treatment plan
(c) The treatment progress
(d) A termination note or treatment summary

The data base section consists of the basic information about the patient necessary before the appropriate treatment plan can be designed. The information is usually acquired through a diagnostic interview (see Chapter III) and may include:

(a) A general information section with the patient's:
   i. Age, sex, ethnic background, and race
   ii. Physical description
   iii. Marital status
   iv. Members of household
   v. Occupation and socioeconomic status
(b) The presenting complaint or reason treatment is sought
(c) A mental health history (a review of previous reasons for seeking treatment, type of treatment obtained, and results)
(d) A mental status evaluation (see Chapter III)
(e) An educational and occupational history
(f) A social history
(g) A medical history or "Review of Systems"
(h) The results of a physical examination and laboratory tests
(i) The problem list (see Chapter V)
(j) The treatment plan (see Chapter V)

A progress note should be written occasionally (ideally, every time the patient is seen) summarizing the current status of the patient's problems and treatments.

At the time of termination some type of closing note should be written. This note may be so brief as to include only the reason for termination or may consist of a review of all the problems, the progress in treatment, and the current status.

The discharge summary, usually required with hospitalized patients, is a closing note that consists of:

(a) Presenting complaint
(b) Psychiatric history
(c) Mental status at the time of admission
(d) Physical exam results
(e) Treatment administered
(f) Changes in the mental status
(g) Discharge plans

The thoroughness of the record varies considerably from one facility to another. The emphasis on good record keeping is growing, however. This emphasis seems appropriate, since a good record:

(a) Forces the therapist to collect and organize all the necessary information about the patient.
(b) Provides a way for others to support or continue the work of the therapist.
(c) Provides the only part of the therapist's work that can be easily scrutinized, as when the records are requested by a court of law.

An example of a complete clinical record is given below. Note that the record belongs to the same patient presented in the example of an interview in Chapter III.

Example of a Clinical Record

Name: Mr. P. Smith   Age: 24
Race: Black
Address: 1224 Orwell Street, Chicago, IL
Phone: 555-1234   Marital Status: Single
Occupation: Unemployed laborer

Presenting Complaint

Mr. Smith stated that he had been hearing voices and feeling like people were making notations about him or changing their conversations when he came by. The patient reported that he started feeling this way about three months ago when he came to the Chicago area seeking employment.

Mental Health History

Mr. Smith stated that he had never received treatment in the past. About one year ago, however, while he was in the military service, he felt that some of his supervisors wanted to get rid of him and deny him—for some unexplainable reason—a military career. He admitted having been in the hospital some time before his discharge from the military service but kept saying that he was only admitted because he needed a brain scan.

Mental Status

Mr. Smith was dressed very neatly and cleanly. He tended to relate in a suspicious and evasive manner, asking the examiner for trivial reassurances before the interview and wanting to know all the specifics of what was about to take place. Obsessive-compulsive traits were evident. Intellectually, the patient appeared to be of normal abilities or slightly below. He was verbal and coherent and able to express himself. There were no indications of intellectual or memory impairments. In his evasiveness, the patient was quite circumstantial, giving all kinds of trivial details and seldom getting down to a clear answer. Some persecutory delusions were noted, and perhaps even some ideas of reference. Although he talked about being persecuted as a response to questioning, he did not appear to be preoccupied with these thoughts and was not fearful. His emotions were appropriate to the content of the conversation, and the prevailing mood was serious but well within the normal limits. The anxiety and activity levels were also normal.

Educational and Occupational History

Mr. Smith dropped out of high school before finishing to enlist in the Air Force. He served in the military for the full four-year term although he apparently had some problems there. Upon discharge he stayed in Michigan, where he had been stationed for nine months, during which time he worked for one day at a department store during the Christmas holidays in his home town. Three months ago he moved to Chicago, where he reportedly has been looking for work unsuccessfully.

Social History

Mr. Smith was brought up in a southern state, the oldest of three children. As a teenager he developed some severe conflict with his parents, since he felt that they favored his youngest sister and were not fair to him. This conflict culminated in his enlistment in the Air Force as a way to get away from the home.

Once in the service he developed some friends but was better characterized as a loner. He blames the isolation on his supervisors, who would give him the type of job that did not have much contact with others. Nevertheless, he was not even able to form relationships with his co-workers. Since his discharge, he has also remained fairly isolated and does not date.

Medical History

During the review of systems, the only medical complaint voiced was that of a recurrent headache during the past few months. He described it as being across the forehead and involving constant pain which increased when he tried to concentrate.

Physical Evaluation

The physical examination revealed a well-nourished 24-year-old black male. Findings of both the physical examination and the Review of Systems were within normal limits except for the presence of a heart murmur.

Problem List

1. Persecutory delusions, ideas of reference

2. Circumstantiality of thought

3. Suspiciousness

4. Lack of social and community resources, lack of job

5. Inability to form relationships

6. Heart murmur

Treatment Plan

1. Supportive treatment—allow patient to feel as comfortable as possible in ward.

2. Medicate (Dr. M. has agreed to prescribe an antipsychotic drug).

3. Attempt to make patient more aware of his problem.

4. Explore possibility of patient returning to home town.

5. If patient intends to stay in area, involve social service and patient in exploring community resources.

6. Make every attempt to set up a milieu in which patient will not be rejected.

7. Assign patient to group therapy and activities and encourage patient to attend.

8. Explore the possibility of involvement in long-term therapy; if possible, find suitable follow-up setting.

Example of a Discharge or Termination Summary

Name: P. Smith   Age: 24
Race: Black
Address: 1224 Orwell Street, Chicago, IL
Phone: 555-1234   Marital Status: Single
Occupation: Unemployed laborer
Diagnosis: Paranoid schizophrenic disorder
Mr. Smith was hospitalized when he developed paranoid delusions and

delusions of reference. The patient claimed to have never received treatment before, but there were indications of poor functioning prior to the present crisis.

Mental Status on Admission

(The previous description would be included here.)

Physical Exam and Lab Reports

(The previous description would be included here, with the abnormal laboratory findings added.)

Course of Treatment

A consultation with Dr. M. led to prescriptions of an antipsychotic medication (Haldol, 10 mg, bid) as well as an anticholinergic drug to take care of side effects (Cogentin, 1 mg, bid). Supportive individual therapy eventually led to the establishment of a trusting relationship between the therapist and the patient. As the patient began to feel more at ease in the ward, he was initiated in a therapy group intended to be supportive and was encouraged to take part in other ward activities.

When substantial improvement had taken place, the patient's family was called. At first they were unenthusiastic at the idea of having the patient back, but their feelings changed through repeated conversations with the staff. It was possible in this way to enlist their cooperation and support.

Mental Status at the Time of Discharge

At the time of discharge Mr. Smith was able to come to the point in his conversations without the trivial details and circumstantiality seen on admission. The persecutory delusions and religious preoccupations had vanished and all other indications of severe emotional disorder had disappeared.

Discharge Plan

Dr. M. provided two weeks of the medications listed above for the patient. Mr. Smith plans to go back to live with his parents. A referral has been made for follow-up treatment at Midway Center. The patient was given an appointment for the initial evaluation on August 30.

TABLE 23. Abbreviations Often Used in Medical Records

Abbreviation	Meaning
AAA	Abdominal aortic aneurysm
abd	Abduct; abdomen
ABG	Arterial blood gas
ac	Before meals

(continued)

TABLE 23. *(continued)*

Abbreviation	Meaning
A.D.	Right ear
ADA	American Diabetic Association
A.D.L.	Activities of daily living
ad lib	As much as needed
AFB	Acid fast bacillus
AICA	Anterior inferior cerebellar artery
A/G	Albumin/globulin ratio
AGN	Acute glomerulonephritis
ALL	Acute lymphocytic leukemia
ALS	Amyotropic lateral sclerosis
AMA	Against medical advice
Amb	Ambulatory
AML	Acute myelocytic leukemia
ANS	Autonomic nervous system
ant	Anterior
AODM	Adult onset diabetes mellitus
A&P	Auscultation and percussion
ARF	Acute respiratory failure
AS	Aortic stenosis
ASAP	As soon as possible
ASHD	Arteriosclerotic heart disease
@	At; each
ATN	Acute tubular necrosis
AVM	Arteriovenous malformation
BE	Barium enema
BK	Below knee
BM	Bowel movement
BNO	Bladder neck obstruction
BP	Blood pressure
BPH	Benign prostatic hypertrophy
BRBPR	Bright red blood per rectum
BRP	Bathroom privileges
BTFU	Bladder tumor follow-up
BUN	Blood urea nitrogen
BX	Biopsy
c	Centigrade
$\bar{c}$	With
Ca	Cancer
CABG	Coronary artery bypass graft
CAD	Coronary artery disease
Cap	Capsule
cbc	Complete blood count

154

TABLE 23. *(continued)*

Abbreviation	Meaning
cc	Cubic centimeters
CC	Chief complaint
CCU	Coronary care unit
CHF	Congestive heart failure
CLL	Chronic lymphocytic leukemia
CML	Chronic myelocytic leukemia
c/o	Complains of
COPD	Chronic obstructive pulmonary disease
CPA	Cerebellopontine angle
CRAG	Cranial radioisotope angiogram
CRF	Chronic renal failure
C&S	Culture & sensitivity
CT	Computed tomography
CVA	Cerebrovascular accident; costovertebral angle
CVP	Central venous pressure
CXR	Chest x-ray
D/C	Discontinue; discharge
D&C	Dilatation and curettage
DIC	Disseminated intravascular coagulation
Diff	Differential
DJD	Degenerative joint disease
DNR	Do not resuscitate
DOA	Dead on arrival
DOE	Dyspnea on exertion
DT('s)	Delirium tremens
DVT	Deep vein thrombosis
DTR	Deep tendon reflex
Dx	Diagnosis
ECG/EKG	Electrocardiogram
ECT	Electroconvulsive therapy
EDV	End diastolic volume
EEG	Electroencephalogram
EF	Ejection fraction
EMG	Electromyography
ENG	Electronystatography
ENT	Ear, nose, and throat
EOM	Extraocular movements
ESR	Erythrocyte sedimentation rate
ESRD	End-stage renal disease
EST	Electroshock therapy
ESV	End systolic volume
ETOH	Ethyl alcohol

(continued)

TABLE 23. *(continued)*

Abbreviation	Meaning
F	Fahrenheit
FABER	Flexion, abduction, external rotation
FBS	Fasting blood sugar
FH	Family history
FS	Frozen section
FUO	Fever of unknown origin
Fx	Fracture
GB	Gall bladder
GC	Gonorrhea
GI	Gastrointestinal
gm	Gram
GMC	General medical clinic
gt	Drop
gtt	Drops
GTT	Glucose tolerance test
GU	Genito-urinary
Gyn	Gynecology
HA	Headache
HCT	Hematocrit
HD	Heart disease
HEU	Health evaluation unit
Hgb	Hemoglobin
HHFM	High-humidity face mask
HJR	Hepato-jugular reflex
H/O	History of
HPI	History of present illness
HTN	Hypertension
HVD	Hypertensive vascular disease
Hx	History
ICCE	Intracapsular cataract extraction
ICP	Intracranial pressure
ICU	Intensive care unit
id	The same
IDDM	Insulin-dependent diabetes mellitus
IG( )	Immunoglobulin (type A,D,E,G, or M)
IHSS	Idiopathic hypertrophic subaortic stenosis
IM	Intramuscular
I&O	Intake & output
IPPB	Intermittent positive pressure breathing
IQ	Intelligence quotient
IR	Internal rotation
IV	Intravenous

156

TABLE 23. *(continued)*

Abbreviation	Meaning
IVP	Intravenous pyelogram
IVPB	Intravenous piggy back
kj	Knee jerk
KUB	Kidney, ureter, and bladder
KV2	Kilivolt
Lat	Lateral
LBBB	Left bundle branch block
LBP	Low back pain
LE	Lower extremity
LIH	Left inguinal hernia
LLL	Left lower lobe
LLQ	Left lower quadrant
LMD	Referring physician
LP	Lumbar puncture
LS	Lumbosacral spine
Lt	Left
LUL	Left upper lobe
MCA	Middle cerebral artery
mEq	Milliequivalent
mg	Milligram
MI	Myocardial infarction
MICU	Medical intensive care unit
mm	Millimeter
MN	Midnight
MOM	Milk of magnesia
MS	Mitral stenosis; multiple sclerosis; mental status
MUGA	Multigated cardiac pool imaging
Mv	Millivolts
n	Noon
NAD	No acute distress
NC	Nasal cannula
Neg	Negative
NG	Nasogastric
NGT	Nasogastric tube
NHP	Nursing home placement
NKA	No known allergies
NPH	Normal pressure hydrocephalus
NPO	Nothing by mouth
NIDDM	Non-insulin-dependent diabetes mellitus
NSR	Normal sinus rhythm
NTG	Nitroglycerine
NTMI	Nontransmural myocardial infarct

(continued)

TABLE 23. *(continued)*

Abbreviation	Meaning
Ob(s)	Obstetrics
OBS	Organic brain syndrome
O.D.	Right eye
OHD	Organic heart disease
OPG	Ophthalmoplethysmography
opth	Ophthalmology
O.S.	Left eye
OT	Occupational therapy
oto	Otology
O.T.	Each eye or both eyes
Path	Pathology
PE	Physical therapy
PERRLA	Pupils equal, round, react to light and accommodation
PFT	Pulmonary function test
PH	Past history
PI	Present illness
PICA	Posterior inferior cerebellar artery
PID	Pelvic inflammatory disease
PMI	Point of maximal impulse
PNB	Prostatic needle biopsy
PND	Paroxysmal nocturnal dyspnea
post	Posterior
PPD	Purified protein derivative
PSVT	Paroxysmal supraventricular tachycardia
PT	Prothrombin time
PTA	Prior to admission
PTH	Parathyroid hormone
PTT	Partial thromboplastin time
PTU	Propylthiouracil
PUD	Peptic ulcer disease
PVC	Premature ventricular contraction
PVD	Peripheral vascular disease
qns	Quantity not sufficient
qs	Quantity sufficient
RAD	Radiation; rads
RBBB	Right bundle branch block
rbc/RBC	Red blood cells
RCM	Red cell mass
RHD	Rheumatic heart disease
RIH	Right inguinal hernia
RLL	Right lower lobe
RLQ	Right lower quadrant

TABLE 23. *(continued)*

Abbreviation	Meaning
RML	Right middle lobe
R/O	Rule out
ROM	Range of motion
ROS	Review of systems
RR	Recovery room
RT	Radiation therapy
rt	Right
RTC	Return to clinic
RUL	Right upper lobe
RX	Take as prescribed
s	Without
SBE	Subacute bacterial endocarditis
SC	Service connected; subcutaneous
SI	Seriously ill
SIADH	Syndrome of inappropriate secretion of antidiuretic hormone
SICU	Surgical intensive care unit
SLE	Systemic lupus erythematosus; slit lamp exam
SMR	Submucous resection
SOB	Shortness of breath
Sol	Solution
s/p	Status post
sp gr	Specific gravity
SSEP	Somatosensory evoked potential
Sx	Symptoms
TB/TBC	Tuberculosis
TBH	Total body hematocrit
T&A	Tonsils and adenoids
T&C	Type & crossmatch
TENS	Transcutaneous electrical nerve stimulation
TIA	Transient ischemic attacks
tko	To keep open
TPR	Temperature pulse respiration
TUR	Transurethral resection
TURP	Transurethral resection of prostate
UA	Urinalysis
UGI	Upper gastrointestinal
URI	Upper respiratory infection
USN	Ultrasonic nebulizer
UTI	Urinary tract infection
U.V.	Ultraviolet
VS	Vital signs
VEA	Ventricular ectopic arrhythmia

(continued)

TABLE 23. *(continued)*

Abbreviation	Meaning
VNA	Visiting Nurse Association
wbc	White blood cells or count
wd	Well developed
wn	Well nourished
WNL	Within normal limits
wt	Weight
$\triangle$	Change
+	Positive
−	Negative
↑	Increase
↓	Decrease
°	Hour; degree
O→	Male
O+	Female

Taken from the list of permissible abbreviations at the Veterans Administration Lakeside Hospital.

VIII Dispositional Decisions

VIII.A. INTRODUCTION

It is extremely important to be able to decide on the type of mental health setting that will best meet a client's needs. In the worst case, dispositional mistakes can lead to the loss of human lives. In less extreme cases, the failure to match patients and settings is still costly, since it leads to early dropouts and failures in therapy.

When determining disposition, it is helpful to consider:

(a) The intensiveness of treatment of the different types of facilities.
(b) The amount of restriction that a particular type of facility places on the patient.

Often these two issues are related, so that the facilities delivering the most intensive treatment (e.g., hospitals) are also the most restrictive. Exceptions are psychoanalysis and psychoanalytically oriented treatments, which may be very intensive but not very restrictive.

The rule of thumb in dispositions is to choose the least intensive and restrictive setting that may fulfill the client's needs. This rule seems appropriate for several reasons. First, it represents a good allocation of professional resources; the more expensive, intensive treatment would be used only when necessary. Second, it avoids giving clients the message that they are sicker than they really are. Finally, it avoids the danger of "institutionalization," having patients regress in an environment where all needs are provided for, where they lose contact with their community and become more uncomfortable with the stresses of daily routines. The prevalent exception to our rule of thumb is, again, the psychoanalytically oriented methods, which may choose to use a fairly intensive treatment with the goal of restructuring the personality of clients who are not very disturbed.

Section VIII.C discusses the different types of mental health facilities. Acquaintance with that material allows the practitioner to choose the least restrictive setting. The present dispositional emphasis is usually to try to avoid hospitalization, since it is probably the most restrictive alternative presently available. There are many times, however, when hospitalization is needed. Good examples of such instances are:

(a) When the patient may be harmful to self or others (see below for further information).

161

    (b) When the patient cannot be handled appropriately outside of the hospital due to:
       i. Intoxication or drug reactions
      ii. Extreme behavioral unpredictability
     iii. Loss of contact with reality that significantly impairs the ability to function, as in the case of some, but not all, hallucinatory or delusional patients
      iv. Extreme behavior, as in a person who is extremely agitated, manic, bizarre, or hostile
    (c) When a person needs an intensive diagnostic workup that may be better done as an inpatient.
    (d) When a client needs a type of treatment that can be done safely only in the hospital. This reason applies mainly to electroconvulsive treatment but may be also be a factor with the administration of psychotropic drugs to an individual who presents some particular medical problems.
    (e) When hospitalization makes sense in terms of a family crisis. (At times, a family may need a "vacation" from the patient, or a family may be showing extreme pathology and having the patient out of the home can help them solve their conflicts.)

The determination of suicidal risk is difficult. Tuckman and Youngman (1968) developed a rating system by taking the risk factors into account. The system works by scoring one point each time that any of the following factors are present:

    (a) Older than 45 years
    (b) Male
    (c) White
    (d) Separated, divorced, or widowed
    (e) Lives alone
    (f) Unemployed or retired
    (g) Poor physical health in past six months
    (h) Mood disorder, alcoholism, or another mental disorder
    (i) Medical care in the last six months
    (j) Firearms, jumping, or drowning used in previous attempt
    (k) Attempt made during warm months
    (l) Attempt made during daylight hours
    (m) Attempt made at own or other's home
    (n) Person reported attempt almost immediately
    (o) Denies intent to kill self
    (p) Left suicide note
    (q) Previous attempts

The scores are then interpreted as follows:

  0-5 Low risk (suicide rate = 6.98/1,000)

  6-9—Medium risk (suicide rate = 19.61/1,000)

  10-12—High risk (suicide rate = 60.61/1,000)

In order to decide on the potential that a particular patient has for harming another person, the professional should take the following into account:

  (a) The amount of anger that the individual shows when talking about it

  (b) How preoccupied the individual is with the issue

  (c) Whether or not the patient is actually threatening to do something

  (d) Whether or not the patient has a plan of action

  (e) Previous history of aggressive acts

  (f) Previous history of impulsive, emotional acts

If the client is judged to be potentially harmful, the professional is morally and legally required to do whatever has to be done in order to assure that everyone involved is safe. For more information about commitment procedures and other legal requirements, see Chapter IX.

VIII.B. THE REFERRAL PROCESS

The referral process involves matching clients with mental health facilities. Even when social workers—who have traditionally been responsible for this part of the treatment—are able to help the client with this task, making appropriate dispositions often requires that the primary therapist be acquainted with the process. What follows are the steps involved in helping a client through this process:

1. Get acquainted with the different types of mental health settings (section VIII.C) as well as with the specific facilities available in the area.

2. Choose the facility that seems to fit best the patient's needs. Make it a cooperative venture that is shared with the patient. In case of doubt, choose the least restrictive facility.

3. Be sure that the client is comfortable with the choice. If not, explore the reasons. Then, either discuss the problems until the client is more comfortable with the decision or consider changing the decision.

4. Be sure that some member of the staff has enough contact with the facility. Be sure that the facility has all the information it needs. Avoid having the staff of this facility feel like you are dumping a patient on them.

Try to make them feel that the referral is made solely on the basis of the patient's needs.

5. Encourage both the patient and the facility to inform you of any difficulties. When difficulties arise, they should be seen as part of a process through which the patient's needs are discovered.

A patient's rejection or return is usually due to one or more of the following:
   (a) The setting to which the patient was referred does not fulfill his or her needs.
   (b) The patient had trouble establishing himself or herself at the center.
   (c) The patient is "acting out."
If the setting was inappropriate, another center should be chosen and the process should be repeated. If the client had trouble getting established, this issue should be addressed in a manner that includes the staff of the new center. Finally, if the client is acting out, the issue has to be explored and understood. Acting out usually is due to the client's dislike for some aspect of the referral. Understanding the dynamic issues involved helps the therapist to decide what course of action to take. It is often appropriate to point out to the client that acting out usually leads to more restrictive and less appropriate dispositions. A new attempt can then be made to involve the client in the decision-making process and have him or her cooperate with the disposition.

VIII.C. MENTAL HEALTH SETTINGS

There are three kinds of mental health facilities:
   (a) Treatment settings
   (b) Placement settings
   (c) Settings that combine treatment and placement (live-in treatment facilities)
Treatment facilities include:
   (a) Private office practices of psychiatrists, psychologists, or social workers. Depending on the office, any of the following may be offered:
      i. Assessments and evaluations
      ii. Individual psychotherapy
      iii. Group psychotherapy
      iv. Family or marital therapy
      v. Drug therapy
   Attention should be paid to the orientation of the therapist. Unfortunately, this type of information is not presently readily available.

(b) Mental hygiene clinics or outpatient clinics, which may employ any one of the mental health professionals and offer any one of the treatments listed above.

(c) Alcoholic treatment programs, usually catering to detoxified, non-psychotic patients who are judged to be motivated to work on their drinking problem.

(d) Drug treatment programs, which are similar to the alcohol treatment programs but are intended for users of other drugs.

(e) Vocational rehabilitation programs, for the evaluation and counseling of clients who have occupational problems.

(f) Day hospital programs, offering structured and therapeutic activities daily for patients who need a program of this type before they can resume a normal life in the community.

(g) Sheltered workshops, geared to patients who need to get back into the routine and responsibility of holding a job or who need a structured life and are not employable.

(h) Sustaining care programs, which are designed for chronic patients who need daily structure and involvement but who are expected to remain at their present level of functioning.

Among the placement settings are the following:

(a) Nursing homes—housing facilities for clients who are psychiatrically or medically disabled.

(b) Retirement homes—facilities for clients who are old but not seriously ill.

(c) Intermediate care facilities—these centers, also called "halfway houses," were originally meant to provide housing during a period of transition after patients were discharged from a hospital but while they were not yet able to resume independent living in the community. Although some continue to function in that manner, most intermediate care facilities also accept patients who are planning to stay there indefinitely.

Live-in treatment facilities include:

(a) Hospital—these facilities are costly and very restrictive to the patient. As a result, they should be used only when they are clearly needed and only for the period of time for which they are needed. Good reasons for hospitalization, however, do exist, as indicated in Section VIII.A. Most hospitals presently have a very brief average length of stay (usually under 30 days). As a result, hospitalization should be seen as a measure to cope with a time of crisis. Occasionally a patient is in definite need of hospitalization for a prolonged period of time. In such a case a hospital must be found that is willing to undertake this task.

(b) Substance abuse detox programs—these facilities give inpatient care for a period of several days for the purpose of detoxifying a patient.

Often, however, they are not equipped to handle patients who present complications (e.g., toxic psychosis, severe medical problems, suicidal risk).

(c) Substance abuse treatment programs—these centers are for patients who are motivated to fight their habit but who, it is believed, would not be able to do so on an outpatient basis. Commonly the programs require that the individual be detoxified before admission.

(d) Vocational rehabilitation programs—these facilities are for clients who are in need of vocational rehabilitation and are so impaired at the present time that they cannot be helped through an outpatient program.

In attempting to offer the best treatment possible, it is often desirable to combine what different facilities have to offer. For instance, a patient may be seeing a private practitioner for emotional problems and going to a vocational rehabilitation program as well. Patients who are sent to intermediate care facilities are often linked to sustaining care programs if a program of that sort does not exist at the intermediate care center. Many more examples could be given. The task of the professional is to set up a program that makes sense for a particular patient; whether this can be done with a single program or with a combination is unimportant.

IX Professional Issues

IX.A. ETHICAL PRINCIPLES

Psychologists are governed by the ethical principles and standards established by the American Psychological Association. What follows is a review of two documents covering this area, "Ethical Principles of Psychologists" (1981) and the *Standards for Providers of Psychological Services* (1984). Only the issues that directly confront students will be discussed here, but readers are strongly encouraged to review the original documents for themselves. Readers involved in computerized testing should also review APA's *Guidelines for Computer-based Tests and Interpretations* (1986).

Responsibility

Psychologists have the duty to use their expertise in a way that protects the welfare of their clients, humanity in general, and the field of psychology. As such, they must minimize the possibility that their findings will mislead and they should take credit only for work that they have actually done. They should avoid relationships that limit their objectivity or create a conflict of interest. Psychologists must take responsibility for their findings and recommendations.

Competence

All clinical work should be performed under the supervision of a psychologist with a doctoral degree and two years of postdoctoral experience. Service providers must keep their knowledge current and not perform jobs for which they are not trained without appropriate supervision.

Supervision

When the person who is delivering the service is not fully trained and qualified to deliver that service, two further issues are present. The first is that of accurate representation: the client has a right to know that the person delivering the service is a trainee. Second, a student's work is appropriate only so long as he or she is adequately supervised. The center and the supervisor, as well as the students, are responsible for taking all measures necessary to assure the adequacy of this supervision.

Public Statements

Psychologists do not misrepresent themselves in any way and should not use sensationalism, exaggeration, or superficiality.

167

Confidentiality

Psychologists are not to reveal any information obtained from a client unless permission is received from that client or unless some other obligation (see below) supersedes this duty. When such information is used in writings or lectures, the professional must either obtain adequate prior consent or disguise all identifying information.

Consumer Welfare

When conflicts of interest arise in the work of a psychologist, he or she has the duty to keep all parties informed of his or her commitments. Every effort should be made to avoid dual relationships that could compromise professional judgment.

Professional Relationships

Psychologists must understand the areas of competence of related professions and not offer their services to individuals who are already receiving similar services from another professional. When contacted by a person who is already receiving similar services, the psychologist must consider both the welfare of the client and the professional relationship involved. When psychologists know of an ethical violation committed by another professional, they are to take steps to implement corrective efforts and handle the information appropriately.

Research

Research is conducted only after all appropriate authorizations have been obtained and informed consent has been secured from the subject.

Accountability

Psychologists must adequately document their evaluations and/or treatment of clients. The cost must be disclosed to the consumer before the service is rendered. Periodic and systematic evaluations of the services provided must be conducted.

IX.B. LEGAL ISSUES

It is of extreme importance for professionals to have some knowledge of the law so that they can operate in a safe and responsible fashion. The material that follows reflects the law in the state of Illinois and may need some alteration to comply with the laws of other states.

Quality of Care

Professionals are legally responsible for delivering the best care they can, in the most "humane" manner, and using the "least restrictive" option possible.

Freedom

At all times clients should have complete freedom to practice their religion and to communicate with whomever they please via mail, telephone, or face-to-face encounters. Patients are to be allowed to possess and use personal property, and live-in centers should provide adequate storage space. A facility, however, can restrict certain objects when this is necessary for the protection of clients.

Informed Consent

Clients have a right to be informed in the most truthful way possible about the following matters:
- (a) The type of treatment being offered
- (b) Alternatives to the treatment being offered
- (c) Their right to refuse treatment
- (d) Their right to consult a lawyer, the Mental Health Advocacy Commission, or anyone else about their treatment

Restriction of Rights

When necessary, in order to prevent clients from causing physical harm to themselves or to others, their rights can be restricted. This restriction usually involves restraints or seclusion of the patient and should be performed according to the following rules:
- (a) The "least restrictive" alternative should always be used.
- (b) A written order must be signed by a physician, if one is available.
- (c) In an emergency when a physician is not available, any qualified person can order the restriction, but this order must be signed by a physician within the next 8 hours.
- (d) No order of this type should be valid for more than 12 hours.
- (e) A person in seclusion must be checked every 15 minutes by a staff person.
- (f) Once a restriction has been employed during a 24-hour period, it cannot be used again during the next two days without written authorization by the facility director.
- (g) Once a restriction has been implemented, the following persons must be informed in writing:

    i. The client

    ii. The facility director

    iii. The parent in the case of a minor, or the guardian in the case of a person under guardianship

    iv. The nearest relative or the person designated by the client to receive such notice

    v. The Mental Health Advocacy Commission if the patient so wishes

The Record

The therapist is required by law to keep a record of the patient's problems, treatment plan, therapy progress, and cost.

The Right to Inspect the Record

Clients, their parents for clients under age 12, their guardians for clients legally incompetent, and the clients' advocates have a right to inspect the clinical record or any information disclosed in the clients' behalf.

The Right to Correct the Record

If the clients or their representatives disagree with some information present in the record, they have a right to have it modified if this is agreeable to the professional who wrote it. Otherwise, they have a right to include a statement in the record that explains their objection.

Confidentiality

Any information given to a professional by a patient or about a patient as part of the treatment process is to be completely confidential and cannot be released to anyone except:

    (a) When the patients, their parents if they are under age 12, or their guardians if they are legally incompetent request information or release of the information. A release must contain:

        i. The patient or agency to whom the disclosure should be made

        ii. The purpose of the disclosure

        iii. The information to be disclosed

        iv. The date or period of time for which the release is valid

    (b) When therapists communicate information to their supervisors, consulting therapists, members of the agency's staff, persons conducting a peer review of the services provided, or the therapists' attorneys when consulting in relation to clients.

    (c) When the court, after giving clients or other interested parties an opportunity to object, orders the professional to release a particular piece of information. (Note that a therapist is not controlled by an ordinary subpoena, which is often obtained without the client's knowledge.)

(d) When the therapist must disclose particular pieces of information in order to prevent harm in cases involving any one of the following:
i. An abused or neglected child
ii. Commitment or competency hearings
iii. Emergency medical care

(e) When the police department wants to know if a particular person is emotionally disturbed in order to determine if that person should be disqualified from owning a gun.

In all cases, only the particular piece of information needed should be disclosed, and a note should be made in the record showing the information disclosed and to whom the disclosure was made.

Commitment or Incompetency

Patients who are dangerous to themselves or to others can be forced to submit to treatment after a court hearing on the matter. The procedure is as follows:

(a) A petition is filled out by any adult who feels that the subject is in need of involuntary hospitalization. A copy of the petition is given to the client, guardian if any, and any two other persons if the client so wishes.

(b) The patient is informed of his or her rights, the purpose of the examinations, and the fact that any information that he or she gives may be used in court to support the need for commitment. Patients should also know that they have a right to legal counsel and are not obligated to talk at all if they do not want to.

(c) A professional (physician, clinical psychologist, psychiatric social worker, or nurse with a master's degree in psychiatric nursing) examines the client to decide if he or she is in fact dangerous to self or others. If the professional decides that this is the case, he or she fills out a certificate testifying to that effect.

(d) A police officer can then be called to transport the patient to a state mental health facility, where the patient will wait for the court proceedings.

(e) Within 24 hours the patient is examined by a psychiatrist, who cannot be the same person who filled out the first certificate. After examining the patient, this psychiatrist fills out a second certificate, also testifying (if this is the case) that the patient is in need of involuntary admission.

(f) All documents are taken to the court at this time. The court must schedule a hearing on the matter within the next five days.

The same procedure should be followed in the case of a person judged to be incompetent or unable to take care of himself or herself or of property.

Admissions

A client in need of inpatient treatment may be admitted to a live-in facility under any of the following contracts:

(a) The informal admission—this type of admission is the least restrictive and should be used whenever it is appropriate. Patients using this type of admission should be informed of their right to be discharged upon request during working hours.

(b) The voluntary admission—this type of admission should be used with a patient who may constitute a danger to self or others but who is willing to apply for admission. A written application form should be used. This type of admission allows the facility to hold the patient for five days after a request for discharge has been received. At the end of that period, if the patient is judged to be potentially harmful, the commitment procedure has to be initiated. Twenty days after admission, the director of the facility has to review the record and request from the patient an affirmation of a wish to stay. The patient's response has to be documented in the record. This procedure then has to be repeated every sixty days thereafter.

(c) Administrative admission—this admission is to be used in the case of a mentally retarded person who is not able to make the decisions involved in requesting admission. The procedure is as follows:

i. The application is filled out by the client if he or she is capable and is 18 years of age or older, by the guardian if the client is incompetent, or by the parent if the client is a minor.

ii. The client is evaluated by a clinical psychologist and a physician; both write reports of their evaluation, recommend an administrative admission (if appropriate), and give their reasons for this recommendation.

iii. The client and any interested person should be told of their right to object to the admission. If they do so, the rules to be followed are the same as those with the voluntary admission contract.

This subject of legal issues in our field is covered in the book by Everstine and Sullivan-Everstine (1986).

IX.C. INSURANCE

Any person who works with patients should be covered under professional liability insurance. This coverage can be obtained individually through the American Psychological Association. In most training centers, however, staff and students are covered under a policy that has been negotiated for the whole center.

References

Ackerman, N. W. (1966). *Treating the troubled family.* New York: Basic Books.

American Medical Association. (1987). *Drug evaluations.* Chicago: Author.

American Psychiatric Association. (1987). *Diagnostic and statistical manual of mental disorders* (3rd ed., revised). Washington, DC: Author.

American Psychological Association. (1981). Ethical principles of psychologists. *American Psychologist, 36,* 633-638.

American Psychological Association. (1984). *Standards for providers of psychological services.* Washington, DC: Author.

American Psychological Association. (1986). *Guidelines for computer-based tests and interpretations.* Washington, DC: Author.

Anrig, G. R. (1987). "Golden Rule": second thoughts. *APA Monitor, 18,* 3.

Aronow, E., & Reznikoff, M. (1976). *Rorschach content interpretation.* Orlando, FL: Grune & Stratton.

Beck, A. T., Rush, A. J., Shaw, B. F., & Emery, G. (1979). *Cognitive therapy of depression.* New York: Guilford Press.

Beck, S. J., Beck, K., Levitt, E., and Molish, H. (1961). *Rorschach's test.* New York: Grune & Stratton.

Bellak, L. (1986). *The T.A.T., C.A.T. and S.A.T. in clinical use* (4th ed.). Orlando, FL: Grune & Stratton.

Bergin, A. E., & Garfield, S. L. (Eds.). (1971). *Handbook of psychotherapy and behavior change: An empirical analysis.* New York: John Wiley.

Berne, E. (1964). *Games people play.* New York: Ballantine Books.

Bernstein, L., Bernstein, R., and Dana, R. (1974). *Interviewing: A guide for health professionals.* New York: Appleton-Century-Crofts.

Blanco, R. G. (1972). *Prescription for children with learning and adjustment problems.* Springfield, IL: Charles C Thomas.

Bowen, M. (1978). *Family therapy in clinical practice.* New York: Jason Aronson.

Brisbane, F. L., & Womble, M. (Eds.). (1985). *Treatment of Black alcoholics.* New York: Haworth Press.

Brodsky, A. M., & Hare-Mustin, R. (Eds.). (1980). *Women and psychotherapy.* New York: Guilford Press.

Bush, W. J., & Waugh, K. W. (1976). *Diagnosing learning disabilities.* Columbus, OH: Charles E. Merrill.

Chessick, R. D. (1974). *Technique and practice of intensive psychotherapy.* New York: Jason Aronson.

Colby, K. M. (1951). *A primer for psychotherapists.* New York: Ronald Press.

Corsini, R. J. (1973). *Current psychotherapies.* Itasca, IL: Peacock.

Cotler, S. B., & Guerra, J. J. (1976). *Assertion training.* Champaign, IL: Research Press.

Curtis, B. A., Jacobson, S., & Marcus, E. M. (1972). *An introduction to the neurosciences.* Philadelphia: W. B. Saunders.

Ellis, A., & Grieger, R. (1977). *Handbook of rational emotive therapy.* New York: Springer.

Erickson, M. H., Rossi, E., & Rossi, S. (1976). *Hypnotic realities.* New York: Irvington Publishers.

Everstine, L., & Sullivan-Everstine, D. (Eds.). (1986). *Psychotherapy and the law.* Orlando, FL: Grune & Stratton.

Exner, J. E. (1974, 1978). *The Rorschach: A comprehensive system* (Vols. 1 and 2). New York: John Wiley.

Exner, J. E., & Weiner, I. B. (1982). *The Rorschach: A comprehensive system* (Vol. 3). New York: John Wiley.

Fabricant, B., & Barron, J. (1977). *To enjoy is to live: Psychotherapy explained.* Chicago: Nelson Hall.

Ferber, A., Mendelsohn, M., & Napier, A. (1972). *The book of family therapy.* New York: Science House.

Filskov, S. B., & Boll, T. J. (Eds.). (1981, 1986). *Handbook of clinical neuropsychology* (Vols. 1 and 2). New York: John Wiley.

Frank, J. D. (1973). *Persuasion and healing* (rev. ed.). Baltimore: Johns Hopkins University Press.

Freedman, A. M., Kaplan, H. I., & Sadock, B. J. (Eds.). (1975). *Comprehensive textbook of psychiatry.* Baltimore, MD: Williams & Wilkins.

Froelich, R. E., & Bishop, F. M. (1977). *Clinical interviewing skills.* St. Louis, MO: C. V. Mosby.

Fromm-Reichmann, F. (1950). *Principles of intensive psychotherapy.* Chicago: University of Chicago Press.

Gardner, E. (1975). *Fundamentals of neurology: A psychophysiological approach.* Philadelphia: W. B. Saunders.

Gender issues in psychotherapy. (1986). *Psychotherapy, 23*(2).

Golden, C. (1985). *Luria Nebraska Neuropsychological Battery.* Los Angeles: Western Psychological Services.

Goldfried, M. R., & Davison, G. C. (1976). *Clinical behavior therapy.* New York: Holt, Rinehart & Winston.

Graham, J. R. (1987). *The MMPI: A practical guide* (2nd ed.). New York: Oxford University Press.

Greene, R. L. (1980). *The MMPI: An interpretative manual.* New York: Grune & Stratton.

Greenson, R. R. (1967). *The technique and practice of psychoanalysis.* New York: International Universities Press.

Gurman, A. S., & Kniskern, D. P. (Eds.). (1981). *Handbook of family therapy.* New York: Brunner/Mazel.

Haley, J. (1963). *Strategies of psychotherapy.* New York: Grune & Stratton.

Haley, J. (1976). *Problem-solving therapy.* San Francisco: Jossey-Bass.

Haley, J., & Hoffman, L. (1967). *Techniques of family therapy.* New York: Basic Books.

Hayes-Roth, F., Longabaugh, R., & Ryback, R. (1972). The problem-oriented medical record and psychiatry. *British Journal of Psychiatry, 121,* 27-34.

Hersen, M., & Turner, S. M. (Eds.). (1985). *Diagnostic interviewing.* New York: Plenum Press.

Horowitz, M., Marmar, C., Krupnick, J., Wilner, N., Kaltreider, N., & Wallerstein, R. (1984). *Personality styles and brief psychotherapy.* New York: Basic Books.

Hubel, D. M., & Wiesel, T. N. (1962). Receptive fields, binocular interaction and functional interaction and functional architecture of the cat's visual cortex. *Journal of Physiology, 160,* 106-154.

Hutt, M. L. (1985). *The Hutt adaptation of the Bender-Gestalt Test* (4th ed.). New York: Grune & Stratton.

Hynd, G., & Obrzut, J. E. (Eds.). (1981). *Neuropsychological assessment and the school-aged child: Issues and procedures.* Orlando, FL: Grune & Stratton.

Jacobson, E. (1964). *Anxiety and tension control: A psychobiological approach.* Philadelphia: Lippincott.

Jarvis, P. E., & Barth, J. T. (1984). *The Halstead-Reitan Test Battery: An interpretative guide.* Odessa, FL: Psychological Assessment Resources.

Jensen, A. R. (1980). *Bias in mental testing.* New York: Free Press.

Johnson, W. R. (1981). Basic interviewing skills. In C. E. Walker (Ed.), *Clinical practice of psychology* (pp. 83-128). New York: Pergamon Press.

Kaplan, H. I., & Sadock, B. J. (Eds.). (1971). *Comprehensive group psychotherapy.* Baltimore, MD: Williams & Wilkins.

Katz, J. E., & Hennessey, M. T. (1981). Which books are perceived helpful in the training of psychotherapists? *Journal of Clinical Psychology, 37,* 505-506.

Kaufman, A. S. (1979). *Intelligent testing with the WISC-R.* New York: John Wiley.

Keyser, D. J., & Sweetland, R. C. (Eds.). (1985-1986). *Test critiques* (Vols. 1-4). Kansas City, MO: Test Corporation of America.

Klopfer, B., Ainsworth, M., Klopfer, W., & Holt, R. (1954). *Rorschach technique.* New York: Harcourt Brace Jovanovich.

Koppitz, E. M. (1963). *Bender Gestalt Test for young children.* Orlando, FL: Grune & Stratton.

Koppitz, E. M. (1967). *Psychological evaluation of children's human figure drawings.* Orlando, FL: Grune & Stratton.

Koppitz, E. M. (1984). *Psychological evaluation of human figure drawings by middle school pupils.* Orlando, FL: Grune & Stratton.

Kramer, C. H., Liebowitz, B., Phillips, R. L., Schmidt, S., & Gibson, J. (1968). *Beginning phase of family treatment.* Chicago: Publications of the Chicago Family Institute.

Lachar, D. (1974). *The MMPI: Clinical assessment and automated interpretation.* Los Angeles: Western Psychological Services.

Lambert, N. M. (1981). Psychological evidence in *Larry P. v. Wilson Riles:* An evaluation by a witness for the defense. *American Psychologist, 36,* 937-952.

Langs, R. (1982). *Psychotherapy: A basic text.* New York: Jason Aronson.

Larry P. v. Riles (October, 1979). U.S. District Court of Northern California, No. C-71-2270.

Lazarus, A. A. (1976). *Multimodal behavior therapy.* New York: Springer.

Leveton, E. (1977). *Psychodrama for the timid clinician.* New York: Springer.

Levinson, D. J. (1978). *The seasons of a man's life.* New York: Ballantine Books.

Levis, D. J. (Ed.). (1970). *Learning approaches to therapeutic behavior changes.* Chicago: Aldine.

Lewis, L., & Swiercinsky, D. (1981). Considerations in referring patients for neuropsychological assessment. *Bulletin of the Menninger Clinic, 45,* 442-446.

Lezak, M. D. (1983). *Neuropsychological assessment* (2nd ed.). New York: Oxford University Press.

Luria, A. R. (1973). *The working brain: An introduction to neuropsychology.* New York: Basic Books.

MacKinnon, R. A., & Michels, R. (1971). *The psychiatric interview in clinical practice.* Philadelphia: W. B. Saunders.

Marks, P. A., Seeman, W., & Haller, D. L. (1974). *The actuarial use of the MMPI with adolescents and adults.* New York: Oxford Press.

Martinez, J. L., & Mendoza, R. H. (Eds.). (1984). *Chicano psychology* (2nd ed.). Orlando, FL: Academic Press.

McGoldrick, M., Pearce, J. K., & Giordano, J. (Eds.). (1982). *Ethnicity and family therapy.* New York: Guilford Press.

Medical Economics. (1987). *Physician's desk reference.* Oradell, NJ: Author.

Megargee, E. I. (1972). *The California psychological inventory.* San Francisco: Jossey-Bass.

Millon, T. (1969). *Modern psychopathology.* Philadelphia: Saunders.

Millon, T., & Millon, R. (1974). *Abnormal behavior and personality.* Philadelphia: Saunders.

Mitchell, J. V. (Ed.). (1985). *The ninth mental measurement yearbook* (Vols. 1 and 2). Lincoln, NE: University of Nebraska Press.

Molyneaux, D., & Lane, V. W. (1982). *Effective interviewing.* Newton, MA: Allyn & Bacon.

Morris, K. T., & Cinnamon, K. M. (1975). *A handbook of non-verbal group exercises.* Springfield, IL: Charles C Thomas.

Neugarten, B. L. (Ed.). (1968). *Middle age and aging.* Chicago, IL: University of Chicago Press.

Oster, G. D., & Gould, P. (1987). *Using drawings in assessment and therapy: A guide for mental health professionals.* New York: Brunner/Mazel.

PASE (Parents in Action on Special Education) *v.* Hannon (August, 1980). U.S. District Court of Northern Illinois, Eastern Division, No. C-74-3586.

Patton, H. D., Sundsten, J. W., Crill, W. E., & Swanson, P. D. (1976). *Introduction to basic neurology.* Philadelphia: W. B. Saunders.

Perls, F. S. (1969). *Gestalt therapy verbatim.* Moab, UT: Real People Press.

Pope, B. (1979). *The mental health interview: Research and applications.* New York: Pergamon Press.

Pruyser, P. W. (1979). *The psychological examination: A guide for clinicians.* New York: International Universities Press.

Reitan, R. M. (1958). The validity of the Trail Making Test as an indicator of brain damage. *Perceptual and Motor Skills, 8,* 271-276.

Reitan, R. M., & Wolfson, D. (1985). *The Halstead-Reitan Neuropsychological Test Battery.* Tucson, AZ: Neuropsychology Press.

Reitan, R. M., & Wolfson, D. (1985). *Neuroanatomy and neuropathology: A clinical guide for neuropsychologists.* Tucson, AZ: Neuropsychology Press.

Reitan, R. M., & Wolfson, D. (1985). *Traumatic brain injury: Pathophysiology and neuropsychological evaluation.* Tucson, AZ: Neuropsychology Press.

Reynolds, C. R., & Gutkin, T. B. (1982). *The handbook of school psychology.* New York: John Wiley.

Rogers, C. R. (1951). *Client centered therapy.* Boston: Houghton Mifflin.

Rogers, C. R. (1967). *On becoming a person.* Boston: Houghton Mifflin.

Sattler, J. M. (1988). *Assessment of children's intelligence* (3rd ed.). San Diego, CA: Jerome M. Sattler, Publisher.

Schontz, F. C. (1982). Adaptation to chronic illness and disability. In T. Millon, C. Green, & R. Meagher (Eds.), *Handbook of clinical health psychology* (pp. 153-172). New York: Plenum Press.

Shaw, D. J. (1966). The reliability and validity of the Halstead Category Test. *Journal of Clinical Psychology, 22,* 176-179.

Singer, E. (1965). *Key concepts in psychotherapy.* New York: Random House.

Strub, R., & Black, F. (1977). *The Mental Status Examination in Neurology.* Philadelphia: F. A. Davis.

Strub, R. L., & Black, F. W. (1981). *Organic brain syndromes: An introduction to neurobehavioral disorders.* Philadelphia: F. A. Davis.

Strupp, H. H., & Binder, J. L. (1984). *Psychotherapy in a new key: A guide to time limited dynamic psychotherapy.* New York: Basic Books.

Sullivan, H. S. (1956). *The psychiatric interview.* New York: W. W. Norton.

Sweetland, R. C., & Keyser, D. J. (Eds.). (1983). *Tests.* Kansas City, MO: Test Corporation of America.

Tallent, N. (1976). *Psychological report writing.* Englewood Cliffs, NJ: Prentice-Hall.

Tomkins, S. S. (1947). *The Thematic Apperception Test.* New York: Grune & Stratton.

Tuckman, J., & Youngman, W. F. (1968). A scale for assessing suicide risk of attempted suicides. *Journal of Clinical Psychology, 24,* 17-19.

Turner, S. M., & Jones, R. T. (1982). *Behavior modification in Black populations: Psychosocial issues and empirical findings.* New York: Plenum.

Vaillant, G. E. (1977). *Adaptation to life.* Boston, MA: Little, Brown.

Watts, T. D., & Wright R. Jr. (1983). *Black alcoholism: Towards a comprehensive understanding.* Springfield, IL: Charles C Thomas.

Whitaker, D. S., & Lieberman, M. A. (1965). *Psychotherapy through the group process.* New York: Atherton Press.

Wolberg, L. R. (1967). *The technique of psychotherapy* (2nd ed.). New York: Grune & Stratton.

Wolman, B. B. (Ed.). (1972). *Manual of child psychopathology.* New York: McGraw-Hill.

Wolpe, J. (1958). *Psychotherapy by reciprocal inhibition.* Stanford, CA: Stanford University Press.

Yalom, I. D. (1985). *The theory and practice of group psychotherapy* (3rd ed.). New York: Basic Books.

Yates, A. J. (1970). *Behavior therapy.* New York: John Wiley.